Current
Controversies
in Alcoholism

The *Advances in Alcohol & Substance Abuse* series:

- *Opiate Receptors, Neurotransmitters, & Drug Dependence:*
  Basic Science-Clinical Correlates

- *Recent Advances in the Biology of Alcoholism*

- *The Effects of Maternal Alcohol and Drug Abuse*
  on the Newborn

- *Evaluation of Drug Treatment Programs*

- *Current Controversies in Alcoholism*

- *Federal Priorities in Funding Alcohol and Drug Abuse Programs*

Current Controversies in Alcoholism

Barry Stimmel, MD, Editor

The Haworth Press
New York

Current Controversies in Alcoholism has also been published as *Advances in Alcohol & Substance Abuse,* Volume 2, Number 2, Winter 1982.

The Haworth Press, Inc., 28 East 22 Street, New York, NY 10010

Library of Congress Cataloging in Publication Data
Main entry under title:

Current controversies in alcoholism.

(Advances in alcohol & substance abuse ; v.2, no. 2)
Bibliography: p.
1. Alcoholism—Addresses, essays, lectures. 2. Alcoholism—Treatment—Addresses, essays, lectures. I. Stimmel, Barry, 1939- . [DNLM: 1. Alcoholism. W1 AD432 v.2, no. 2 / WM 274 C976]
HV5035.C87   1983   362.2'92   83-207
ISBN 0-86656-225-7

Current Controversies in Alcoholism

Advances in Alcohol & Substance Abuse
Volume 2, Number 2

CONTENTS

EDITORIAL: The Importance of Scientific Controversy   1
Barry Stimmel, MD

The Rand Reports Reviewed: A Critical Analysis   7
Harry Smith, PhD
George Jackson, MD

Patients Who Refuse Study: A Bias Factor in Alcoholism
Prevalence Research   17
Thomas P. Beresford, MD
Dennis Low, MD
Richard C.W. Hall, MD

Group Therapy with Alcoholic Clients: A Review   23
Sandra C. Anderson, PhD

General Indicators of Alcohol-Related Mortality for United
States Counties   41
Robert A. Wilson
Edward C. Ratledge
Henry J. Malin

Marijuana Use in Alcoholism: Demographic Characteristics
and Effects on Therapy   53
David Benzer, DO
Paul Cushman, Jr., MD

Alcohol Use during Pregnancy: What Advice Should Be
Given to the Pregnant Woman?   61
David B. Roll, PhD
Terrence Smith, MPA
Elizabeth M. Whelan, ScD

Selective Guide to Current Reference Sources on Topics
Discussed in this Issue   69
            Theodora Andrews

Information for Authors   81

Current Controversies in Alcoholism

EDITORIAL

The Importance
of Scientific Controversy

Controversy is essential to science. It is the validation and reval-
idation of hypotheses that allow advances in both the social and
the biological sciences. Although the biology of alcoholism and its
toxic effects have been relatively well defined, advances are still
being made and, especially with respect to their clinical relevance,
much controversy prevails. In the clinical sphere of alcoholism,
however, there is, understandably, far less precision in validating
hypotheses, although views are expressed with an equal if not
greater enthusiasm.

This issue of *Advances* addresses several of the more controversial or, perhaps, less well proven issues in the field of alcoholism.
The lead paper by Smith and Jackson[1] provides a critical review of
the Rand Reports,[2,3] a series of publications dealing with one of
the few multicenter studies attempting to define the prognosis of
alcoholism. When the first Rand Report was published more than
five years ago, considerable controversy ensued. The findings
were alleged to have promoted social drinking among former alcoholics and to have demonstrated that no treatment was "effective
treatment." The second Rand Report, extending the follow-up period, has been purported to invalidate the findings of the first,
illustrating that alcoholics cannot be social drinkers and that intervention is effective in averting the known complications of alcoholism. In fact, as discussed by Smith and Jackson, the Rand Reports neither made such initial claims nor later refuted their
original findings. Although the selection of the study population

was far from random, nonetheless, the investigators methodically followed their subjects, developed a data base, and were quite careful in stating the limitations and caveats associated with their findings. They acknowledged that they did not prove social drinking a viable option for former alcoholics and that their study design did not allow a comparison of treatment versus nontreatment.

It is important to emphasize that the controversy following the publication of the first Rand Report in fact had much earlier origins, reflecting the intense feelings surrounding social drinking in alcoholics often found among professionals in the field of alcoholism. Davies,[4] in 1962, reported 7 of 93 former alcoholics able to drink moderately on long-term follow-up. These findings were confirmed and extended by Sobell and Sobell[5,6] and Caddy et al[7] who demonstrated a better long-term follow-up among alcoholics trained in controlled drinking than those treated in a traditional abstinence model. The question of social drinking by former alcoholics, however, remains controversial. Pendery et al,[8] reviewing the initial report by the Sobells, have alleged that the controlled drinking subjects failed from the outset, with only one of the original 20 subjects able to successfully control his alcohol intake. An independent committee has been formed to review these data to determine the accuracy of the initial findings. As of the present, it must be accepted that there is no firm evidence to indicate that former alcoholics can drink socially, although surely the possibility may exist.[9] Further well-designed studies are needed if this question is to be answered satisfactorily.

The importance of a suitable study design and a random selection of persons participating in any study is emphasized by the second paper by Beresford et al.[10] In a small survey of general hospital patients who refused to consent to participate in an alcoholism survey, the prevalence of alcoholism was nearly twice that seen among the patients agreeing to participate. The overall prevalence of alcoholism in the study population increased by more than 25% when the nonparticipating alcoholics were included. This does not suggest the futility of initiating a study unless all potential subjects agree to participate. A recent publication has demonstrated that meaningful data can be obtained even when a considerable number of individuals choose not to participate, providing the characteristics of the nonparticipants and the participants are similar.[11] It is essential, however, that these two groups are carefully reviewed so that any bias that may exist can be rapidly identified.

Anderson[12] reviews the existing literature on group therapy for alcoholics, exploring the rationale that has allowed group therapy to become one of the most accepted forms of treatment for alcoholism. However, although a favorable consensus exists concerning its effectiveness, there is little validation of this in the literature, and there have been no well-designed prospective studies to test its effectiveness. Considering the funding that has gone into the development of such programs, allocation of even 2% of these funds would allow this issue to be addressed.

It is the general consensus that there are approximately ten million alcoholics in this country, with three times as many indirectly affected by alcohol use. These figures, however, are quite "soft" and cannot withstand scrutiny. Although many indicators have been used in an attempt to define prevalence, nonetheless, we have been relatively unsuccessful in providing any other than a gross estimate. The paper by Wilson et al[13] reviews the relationships among several of the more commonly utilized prevalence indicators. They suggest that the use of combined indices reflecting mortality indicators, alcohol-related health problems, homicides, alcohol-related accidents and suicides allows a greater degree of accuracy than addressing this problem through individual mortality variables, as is commonly done. These views deserve further scrutiny.

The extent to which alcoholics abuse or misuse other drugs has always been of concern. Since alcohol belongs to the group of drugs consisting of barbiturates, hypnotics, sedatives and minor tranquilizers, it is not surprising that the use of these substances by alcoholics is considerable. At times, this use has been fostered by physicians in the mistaken impression that the treatment of an alcoholic with a benzodiazephine will relieve the alcoholism, enabling the individual to become more functional. This, unfortunately, is far from true. Alcohol may be easily interchanged with any of the drugs in this group with a mood-altering effect quite acceptable to the alcoholic.

The use of other mood-altering drugs by alcoholics, however, has received less scrutiny. Benzer and Cushman,[14] in a moderately sized study of marijuana use by alcoholics, have found that almost 30% of clients admitted to an alcohol treatment program had a positive urine screen for THC on admission, with more than three-quarters of this group admitting use of marijuana just prior to their interview. Although experience suggests that polydrug use is associated with a poorer response to treatment, the use of marijuana did not appear to significantly impact on successful engagement in therapy. However, this retrospective study does not really address treatment outcome. It would be quite hazardous to assume that recreational use of marijuana in alcoholics does not effect the rehabilitative process, or that recreational use would not increase considerably as alcohol consumption diminishes if emergent anxieties are not addressed.

Few recent findings have generated as much concern and controversy in the field of alcoholism as the recognition of the fetal alcohol syndrome (FAS) and the subsequent recommendations of the National Institute on Alcohol Abuse and Alcoholism concerning prohibitions to be placed on even minimal drinking by pregnant women. While the existence of this syndrome is beyond doubt, its prevalence and the amount of alcohol that can be safely consumed during pregnancy without risk remain open to question. It belabors the obvious to state that pregnant women should refrain from consuming any substances other than those necessary for nutrition. Nonetheless, there are a considerable number of pregnant women who drink sporadically or, more importantly, had been social drinkers prior to their being aware either of the FAS or of their pregnancy. As discussed by Roll et al,[15] the development of an arbitrary safety standard can do much psychological harm to those women who have consumed small amounts of alcohol and are not at risk of developing the FAS. In fact, as noted by these authors, the prevalence of this syndrome in some studies strains credibility. Since many variations of the FAS are being reported, it is conceivable that some observations made in a number of these infants are unrelated to maternal alcohol consumption. The true prevalence of the FAS needs further study, and the reasons for setting specific limits for safe consumption of alcohol require further explanation.

The papers presented in this issue may raise more questions than they answer. This is appropriate. Only through critically evaluating data can knowledge be refined and advanced. Faith in one's belief is important in the verification process only in so far as it becomes a motivating force toward scientific inquiry. Uncritical acceptance serves neither the clinician nor the patient and must be avoided by those engaged in research as well as the provision of care.

Barry Stimmel, MD

REFERENCES

1. Smith H, Jackson G. The Rand Reports reviewed: a critical analysis. Advances in Alcohol & Substance Abuse. 1982; 2:7-15.
    2. Armor DJ, Polich JM, Stambul HB. Alcoholism and treatment. New York: John Wiley and Sons, 1978.
    3. Polich JM, Armor DJ, Braiker HB. The course of alcoholism: four years after treatment. The Rand Corp. R-2423-NIAAA, Santa Monica, California, 1980.
    4. Davies DL, Shepherd M, Myers E. Two years' prognosis of 50 addicts after treatment in hospital. QJ Study Alcohol. 1956; 17:458-502.
    5. Sobell MB, Sobell LC. Alcoholics treated by individualized behavior therapy: one year treatment outcome. Behav Res Ther. 1973; 11:599-618.
    6. Sobell MB, Sobell LC. Behavioral treatment of alcohol problems: individualized therapy and controlled drinking. New York: Plenum Press, 1978.
    7. Caddy GR, Addington HJ, Perkins D. Individualized behavior therapy for alcoholics: a third year independent double-blind follow-up. Behav Res Ther. 1978; 16:345-62.
    8. Pendery ML, Maltzman IM, West LJ. Controlled drinking by alcoholics? New findings and a reevaluation of a major affirmative study. Science. 1982; 217:169-75.
    9. Gottheil E, Thornton CC, Skdoda TE. Follow-up of abstinent and nonabstinent alcoholics. Am J Psychiatry. 1982; 139: 560-65.
    10. Beresford TP, Low D, Hall RCW. Patients who refuse study: a bias factor in alcoholism prevalence research. Advances in Alcohol & Substance Abuse. 1982; 2:17-22.
    11. Stimmel B, Hanbury R, Sturiano V, Korts D, Jackson G, Cohen M. Alcoholism as a risk factor in methadone maintenance: a randomized control trial. Am J Med. In Press.
    12. Anderson SC. Group therapy with alcoholic clients: a review. Advances in Alcohol & Substance Abuse. 1982; 2:23-40.
    13. Wilson RA, Ratledge EC, Malin HJ. General indicators of alcohol-related mortality for United States counties. Advances in Alcohol & Substance Abuse. 1982; 2:41-52.
    14. Benzer D, Cushman P Jr. Marijuana use in alcoholism: demographic characteristics and effects on therapy. Advances in Alcohol & Substance Abuse. 1982; 2:53-60.
    15. Roll DB, Smith T, Whelan EM. Alcohol use during pregnancy: what advice should be given to the pregnant woman? Advances in Alcohol & Substance Abuse. 1982; 2:61-67.

The Rand Reports Reviewed:
A Critical Analysis

Harry Smith, PhD
George Jackson, MD

ABSTRACT. Considerable controversy concerning the effectiveness of treatment for alcoholism and the ability of alcoholics to come social drinkers has been generated by the publication of the Rand Reports of 1975 and 1980. The 1980 Report describes the outcome of a cohort of 922 alcoholics followed for four years after initiating contact at an alcoholic treatment center. A critical review of the study design analytic methods and results reveals the authors to have seriously addressed the statistical problems as well as clearly stating the contraints that should be utilized in interpreting their findings.

Although the sampling selection of the final cohort leads to bias, nonetheless the results presented are of interest. The results do not indicate either that different types of treatment are equally effective or that alcoholics may safely resume social drinking. The descriptive findings of the selective cohort, however, suggest that these observations should be studied prospectively under randomized controlled conditions.

To attempt a long-term longitudinal study on patients who contact an Alcoholic Treatment Center (ATC) at least once is at the best hazardous. The Rand studies[1,3] illustrate how difficult and time consuming it is to maintain a good follow-up on a large number of patients. In this respect, the study team did an outstanding job and are to be commended for their tenacity and hard work. They have been very careful in identifying the caveats of the

The authors are affiliated with the Departments of Biomathematical Science and Community Medicine, The Mount Sinai School of Medicine of the City University of New York. Address reprints to: Harry Smith, PhD, Chairman, Department of Biomathematical Science, Mount Sinai School of Medicine, One Gustave L. Levy Place, New York, New York 10029.

We would like to acknowledge the thoughtful comments of Dr. Susan D. Solomon at the National Institute on Alcohol Abuse and Alcoholism.

study, but unfortunately, the majority of workers in the field may easily overlook the caveats and make generalizations to their treatment situation. As a result both the initial study[1] and the subsequent one[3] have generated considerable controversy concerning the effectiveness of treatment in alcoholism as well as the possibility for alcoholics to become social or nonproblem drinkers.

The purpose of this paper is to review critically this latest report by Polich et al.[3] and to comment on its implications for the treatment of alcoholics. This review will focus first on the study design and its resultant limitations and second on the conclusions of the study with respect to treatment implications.

THE STUDY DESIGN AND METHODS

The 1980 report is a nonexperimental study of 922 male alcoholics who contacted one of eight alcoholic treatment centers (ATC) excluding all contacts who were classified as driving while intoxicated (DWI). This is a continuation of the 18 month following-up study reported by W. Lee Ruggels et al.[1,2] in 1975. Thus, any limitations of that study will apply to this one. The sampling frame in the 1980 report is not clear to us. It was necessary to return to the 1975 report to clarify the design frame and attempt to reconstruct the base from which the 922 males were obtained. While the 1975 report is very clear, the transition from it to the present study is not. However, a number of limitations are apparent.

The eight ATCs studied (Baltimore, Orlando, Pine Bluff, San Antonio, Fort Worth, Fort Dodge, Phoenix and San Jose) were volunteer units willing to participate out of a population of 44 ATCs nationwide. They represent a very limited geographical base for inference since there were no Northeast or North Central ATCs represented. There were very big differences from clinic to clinic of both relevant patient characteristics and drink-related behavior at intake. It was quite difficult to determine the relationship between the 18-month study group and the 4-year study group, i.e., the origin of the 922 patients reported in the long-term follow-up. It appears that these patients are a very select subset which does not allow for generalized inferences based on subsequent findings. While the data indicate that overall patient characteristics at intake were close to those of the whole population of patients at the 44 ATCs, caution is warranted as the conclusions of the study are heavily weighted by patients from southern ATCs.

One of the major problems in assessing the outcome of a long-term study is the bias introduced due to patient attrition secondary to withdrawal, death, or failure to be located. The characteristics of those persons completing the study compared to those failing to complete become as important as the actual retention or completion rate. Given that the samples were selected as indicated, Polich et al. did a superb job, achieving an overall completion rate of 85%. However these patients really represented a proportion of those who entered the 1975 study which had an 18-month completion rate of 57.8%. If one appropriately uses this original sampling frame to avoid bias, then the overall completion rate diminishes considerably.

The comparison analysis of admission characteristics of completed versus noncompleted cases (Table 1) as reported indicated small differences except for a higher mobility among the noncompleted cases. However, one must be impressed by the fact that the percentages for all reported characteristics were uniformly higher in the noncompleted cases compared to the completed cases. Once again, it is difficult to assess whether this is critical or not, since these characteristics are not uncorrelated and one cannot

TABLE 1

Characteristics of Four Year Follow-Up Groups on
Admission to Treatment by Retention Program

	Percent with Characteristic	
	Completed Cases (n = 645)	Noncompleted Cases (n = 113)
Age 50 or over	43	46
Alcohol Consumption over 5oz. per day	58	65
High symptomatology	79	87
Less than 4 years in community	42	56
Low socioeconomic status	45	50
Low social stability	44	50
Previously treated for alcoholism	42	46

From Polich et al.[2]

determine their simultaneous effect on the potential bias of study results. However, looking at these univariate results, the completed cases would seem to be younger, less mobile, somewhat higher in socioeconomic level and social stability, consume less alcohol, have better symptomatology and have fewer previous treatments for alcoholism. While we do not necessarily agree with these conclusions, presenting univariate tables leads one to such inferences and may be potentially misleading. The data suggest therefore that those patients completely followed for four years are in fact a very select subset of patients.

DEFINING TERMS

Since so many of the conclusions of the study are based on the definition of "problem drinking," a brief discussion of the drinking definitions is needed. The 1980 Rand Report uses four categories: Long-term Abstainers (six months or more), Short-term Abstainers (one to five months), Normal Drinking (drinking with no symptoms) and Nonremission (drinking with symptoms). These definitions represent a tightening up of the nonproblem drinking categories when compared to the 18-month study when "normal" drinking allowed some alcohol symptomatology. In the 1980 study "normal drinking" allowed *no* alcoholic synptomatology, no continuous drinking over 12 hours at a time and no adverse consequences of drinking such as alcoholic related diseases, legal problems, and work-related problems such as fights, unemployment, etc. This was an excellent change of definition allowing a clear separation between excessive alcohol consumption and social "normal" drinking.

MAJOR FINDINGS

The Effect of Therapy

This study was not designed to compare different treatment modalities. Thus, any conclusions indicated are subject to all kinds of interpretation. The results should be treated as hypotheses formulations only. The study found a modest correlation between the amount of treatment that a patient received and the patient's condition at follow-up. No correlation favoring one particular type of treatment over another (e.g., outpatient versus inpatient) was observed. The study has the very serious limitation of studying a self-selected group of patients, and it is not surprising to us that there is substantial improvement even among those patients treated minimally. As the authors state, to generalize from this finding by saying outpatient care is as good as inpatient care would be incorrect. Possible therapeutic implications of these findings can only be assessed through randomized controlled studies.

Short-Term Abstention as a Form of Remission

By dividing drinkers into the four categories: short-term abstainers, long-term abstainers, normal drinkers (no alcoholic symptoms) and nonremission drinkers, the Rand study demonstrated the similarities between long-term abstainers and normal drinkers and between short-term abstainers and nonremission drinkers. For example, of those patients classified as long-term abstainers and normal drinkers at 18 months, 3% died from alcohol-related diseases during the subsequent 30 month follow-up period. The short-term abstainer and nonremission group had a 9% death rate during the same 30 months. In addition, the report indicates that most short-term abstainers (one to five months) report serious alcoholic symptomatology. Short-term abstention is therefore not prognostic of a stable positive status.

After allowing for the basic study limitations, one easily concludes that the typical 30-day window frequently used to determine alcoholic treatment outcomes must be reassessed. The data are very persuasive on this point. The conclusion is that a minimum of six months follow-up is needed, although the cost of doing this may be prohibitive. Unfortunately, the study was unable to determine if the short-term abstainer subset was basically different from the long-term abstainer subset. Since every long-term abstainer must past through the short-term abstainer class, why were these groups prognostically incompatible? Further research is needed on this important point.

Social Drinking as a Possible Alternative for the Alcoholic

This study demonstrates that the relapse rates were "somewhat lower for long-term abstainers than for nonproblem drinkers, although the difference was not statistically significant." "Among people who were under 40, unmarried, or less dependent on alcohol at admission, the rate of relapse for nonproblem drinkers was equal or lower than the rate for long-term abstainers. Hence, it appears that for some alcoholics, especially those under 40 and less dependent on alcohol, nonproblem drinking can be regarded as a form of remission." Here we part company with the Rand Report. The analytical techniques used to come to this conclusion are multivariate in nature—the result of a model building process using logit regression analysis. The R^2, the percentage of variation in the data explained by the model, is only 13.5% in one case and 7.2% in the other comparison. While coefficients within each model can be statistically significant, these models are grossly inadequate for convincing anyone.

To further compound the problem, the authors calculate estimated relapse rates using the two different models. It is not clear if these models consist of all 19 variables or only those variables whose fitted coefficients were statistically significant.

As a kind of guideline for determining model utility, the R^2 statistic is commonly used. Given that the sample size n is at least ten times the number of variables in the ultimate model, the physical sciences expect R^2 to be greater than 90%; the biological and economic sciences require an R^2 between 50 and 80%, while the social sciences (the case here) usually expect R^2 to be in excess of 25%.

The authors have employed extremely powerful statistical techniques with a large sample size and have obtained statistically significant results. However, the model is not significant enough to convince us that this result will necessarily hold up under scientific replication. The idea is an intriguing one, and like Polich et al., we hope that it will be given a more rigorous test in future work.

One other point needs to be made about the relapse analysis. Transition relapse rates are indicated for two time periods: 6 months - 18 months - 4 years. It would have been useful if the authors had used Markov chain theory to test the stable transition rate hypotheses. For the 169 patients followed in all three periods this would have been possible. The analysis presented is not adequate to make statements like "the considerable instability of status is such that the time between 6 months and 18 months may be too short to establish long-term relapse patterns."

Changes in Psychosocial Functioning

The Rand Report found a poor relationship between objective social stability measures and drinking status at four years, with any progress observed essentially unrelated to drinking status. Regardless of improvement in drinking behavior, active rehabilitation was rarely achieved. Once again maladjustment was greatest among problem drinkers and short-term abstainers with long-term abstainers or nonproblem drinkers exhibiting the greatest improvements in psychosocial functioning. However, the data presented are univariate, and there is no way to determine what percent of the people who were employed at the beginning stayed employed throughout, what percent moved from employment to unemployment, etc. Thus the transition data were not shown. This could have been done for the social stability variables. The psychiatric variables, general life conditions personality characteristics, etc., were done only at the 4-year follow-up period. The authors correctly warn the reader that ". . . the psychosocial characteristics of our respondents will be treated only as correlates of the follow-up categories. As such, their status as etiological factors in alcoholism, as prognostic indicators of treatment outcomes, or simply as consequences of drinking or abstention must remain ambiguous pending further research."

The statistical work pertaining to psychosocial functioning is sophisticated and well-done up to a point, although the authors were using seven groups for initial analysis instead of the final four groups for which the ultimate conclusions were drawn. The statistical tools used to relate psychosocial variables to 4-year follow-up status groups were first, discriminant analysis to define dimensionality, then rotated discriminant coefficients for interpreting the results. Thus, the authors started with a large number of items, first reduced by creating scales on general areas like Mental Health, etc., then using discriminant analysis reduced these general areas to two indices: (1) ". . . Perception of harm from future drinking and, less strongly, by the alcoholic self-concept item; and (2) a mental health dimension."

While each of these two indices is statistically significant, no indication is shown how really good these two rotated discriminant indices are. For example, if one uses these to predict the group to which an individual belongs, what would the misclassification percentage be and to which groups would group members be assigned? The reader is never given any indication of the practical utility of these results.

SUMMARY

Polich et al. applied themselves diligently to both data handling and statistical analysis. In retrospect, one would have been more comfortable if the original study design had included a data window at four points in time: baseline, 6 months, 18 months, and four years, with the same amount of effort to obtain complete follow-up throughout the four years. However, in analyzing the data when several techniques were possible, this team did all of them, frankly reporting their consistencies and inconsistencies. Techniques used ranged from simple univariate statistics to sophisticated multivariate techniques. While we have disagreed with the use of some of these statistical results, we find no problem with the techniques themselves. Although additional results showing the inadequacy of the models could have been done, in general the statistical work was excellent.

Overall Conclusion

The authors were also explicitly cautious in drawing conclusions. If the reader considers all the caveats in the report, no one can really criticize the findings. They represent the facts as they were obtained, subject to all the constraints expressed above. There is much "food for thought." Since the prognosis for the non-problem drinker tended to be closer to the long-term abstainer, the role of alcoholic symptomatology in the prognosis of the treatment of alcoholics needs to be carefully examined. Even within the constraints of the study these findings are of interest. Their ideas and conjectures need further study and replication in carefully designed experiments. Should a nonproblem drinker be considered an alcoholic in remission? Is it possible? Or is abstinence the only societal solution? Much work needs to be done. We believe the National Institute of Alcohol Abuse and Alcoholism sponsored work so admirably done by Polich et al. deserves a great deal of credit. The report provides physicians who treat alcoholics and researchers who study alcoholism with many ideas, most of which are supported by observations in this report and all of which can be tested by vigorously designed controlled studies.

REFERENCES

1. Ruggels WL, Armour DJ, Polich MJ, Mothershead A, Stephen M. A follow-up study of clients at selected alcoholism treatment centers. Funded by NIAAA. Menlo Park, California. Stanford Research Institute, 1975.

2. Armor DJ, Polich JM, Stambul HB. Alcoholism and treatment. New York: John Wiley and Sons, 1978.

3. Polich, JM, Armor DJ, Braiker, HB. The course of alcoholism: four years after treatment. The Rand Corporation, R-2423-NIAAA, 1980.

Patients Who Refuse Study: A Bias Factor in Alcoholism Prevalence Research

Thomas P. Beresford, MD
Dennis Low, MD
Richard C.W. Hall, MD

ABSTRACT. The authors report a study of 33 general hospital patients who refused consent for an alcoholism survey. They note suspected alcoholism prevalence rates of 62% among the medical patients and 45% among the orthopedic surgery patients who refused study inclusion. The suspected prevalence rate among medical service patients was nearly twice that found among medical service patients who accepted inclusion in the authors' survey. Estimates of total prevalence were approximately 10% greater when patients from the refusal group, who were suspected of alcoholism, were included. The total estimated number of alcoholism patients increased by 26% when the refusal group patients were included. The authors suggest ways of systematizing data from patients who refuse inclusion in clinical studies.

Subjects lost to clinical research are a significant and as yet poorly studied source of bias in assessing research results. Koran and Costell reviewed factors contributing to early termination in a prospective study of psychotherapy groups. They found that patients who failed to complete or refused to complete questionnaires designed to probe feelings, personality, and projected group behavior were very likely to leave the group therapy early.[1]

Thomas P. Beresford is Chief, Psychiatry Service, Veterans Administration Medical Center and Associate Professor of Psychiatry, University of Tennessee College of Medicine. Dennis Low is Assistant Director of Primary Care, Department of Medicine, Santa Clara Valley Medical Center, San Jose, CA. Richard C. W. Hall is Chief of Staff, Veterans Administration Medical Center, and Professor of Psychiatry and Internal Medicine, University of Tennessee College of Medicine, Memphis. Direct requests for reprints to: Thomas P. Beresford, M.D., Department of Psychiatry (116A), Veterans Administration Medical Center, 1030 Jefferson Avenue, Memphis, Tennessee.

Kokes and co-workers investigated subject refusal by comparing 50 psychiatric patients who refused to participate in research interviews and psychological tests with a control group who agreed to research involvement.[2] No statistically significant differences were seen between the two groups in regard to demography, hospitalization, or the type or degree of pathology. However, their data showed that a patient's willingness to be included in the psychiatric study depended upon the amount of his or her prior institutional contact and the severity of the specific disorder in the investigational design. Kokes and colleagues concluded that selection on the basis of patient consent is a significant bias in clinical research.

We recently completed a clinical study assessing alcoholism prevalence on general medical and orthopedic services of a county hospital.[3] Because of the potentially controversial nature of a study of alcoholism among medical inpatients in a public hospital setting, we were required by our institutional review board to include a patient consent form that would ensure informed acceptance or refusal of our interview. The consent form established that the investigators would ask the patient for basic demographic data, data on past psychiatric history and drug use, and four alcoholism screening questions. Depending on factors related to the study design, the questionnaire also stated that detailed questions about alcohol use might also be included. A significant percentage of patients who were approached refused to participate in the study. The present investigation was designed to assess the effects of the subject refusal as a potentially biasing factor in estimates of alcoholism prevalence.

Method

We approached patients admitted consecutively to general medical and orthopedic surgery wards and asked them to participate in an alcoholism prevalence survey. Patients who refused to participate were asked to state their objections verbally in a sentence or two. The patient's reasons were then recorded by the investigator. Our study design, approved by the institutional review board of our medical center, included a review of each patient's medical chart prior to the initial contact. Following completion of the survey, we conducted a more systematic record review of patients who refused study as well as of those who had agreed to inclusion.

The data reported here were gathered on these occasions. At the first review, we were blind to the patient's acceptance or refusal. At the more detailed review, we made no attempt to segregate the records of accepting or refusing patients but recorded the chart data as the records were presented to us. We specifically noted (1) a prior history of alcohol diagnosis or suspected alcohol diagnosis on the part of a physician who examined the patient, (2) the presence of alcohol-related illnesses, and (3) the presence of physical stigmata of chronic alcohol use such as liver enlargement, spleen enlargement, and angiomata. We also noted histories of drug abuse and psychiatric hospitalization. We evaluated these data in two ways. First, we divided the refusal group into those who had a significant alcohol abuse history and those who did not. We then examined differences of patients who had refused participation and who presented a history of alcohol abuse with those who had agreed to participate in the study and also had a history of alcohol abuse.

Results

Of 232 possible subjects in our study, 199 accepted inclusion and 33 did not. Of the 33 patients who who refused consent for the study, 22 were men and 11 were women. Twenty of the patients were admitted to the medicine service and 13 to the orthopedic surgery service. The mean age of the refusal group was 46.1 years, ranging from 20 to 79 years. These demographic data did not statistically separate the refusal group from the consent group. At interview, 17 of the 33 patients who refused inclusion (52%) gave no explanation as to the reason for the refusal (Table 1). Another 8 patients (24%) stated that they felt the questions we wished to ask would be too personal. Two patients each (6%) felt that they were either too ill, were under legal duress, or were suspicious of research studies. The final two patients gave specific reasons: "I don't drink" and "Father was a drunk and I don't want to talk about such things."

We reviewed the medical charts for 32 of the 33 refusal patients. Eighteen of the 32 patients met one or more of the criteria indicating suspected alcohol abuse. Twelve of the suspected alcohol abuse group (65%) presented physical illnesses related to alcohol use. Four of this group (22%) presented histories of seizures related to alcohol withdrawal. Two patients (11%) gave a history

TABLE 1

REASONS FOR STUDY REFUSAL

(N = 32)

REASON	n	SUSPECTED ALCOHOLISM (N = 18)	NON-SUSPECTED (N = 14)
1. No explanation	16	10	6
2. Too personal	8	7*	1*
3. Too ill	2	0	2
4. Legal implications	2	1	1
5. Suspicious of consent forms	2	0	2
6. "I don't drink"	1	0	1
7. "Father was a drunk"	1	0	1

* frequencies differ significantly, $p < 0.05$

of polydrug abuse, and one patient presented a past history of psychiatric hospitalization (6%). By comparison, only one (7%) of the nonalcoholic group of patients who refused the study presented a seizure history and one patient (7%) presented a history of psychiatric hospitalization. The suspected alcoholism group presented the following physical findings on their admission examination: hepatomegaly (39%), angiomata (22%), ascites (11%), jaundice (11%), testicular atrophy (11%), and splenomegaly (6%). None of the nonalcoholic group who refused study inclusion presented any of these signs.

Table 1 compares the two refusal groups with regard to their reasons for refusing inclusion in the study. Almost all of the patients suspected of alcohol abuse gave no explanation or said that the information we requested was too personal. The majority of the nonalcoholic refusal patients gave no explanation; only one patient said that our questions were too personal. The frequency difference for the "too personal" response between the two groups was statistically significant (two-tailed binomial test, p < 0.05).

We next compared these data with those gleaned from interviews and chart reviews of those patients who accepted inclusion in the study. The frequencies of alcohol-related illnesses, seizures, drug abuse and psychiatric histories, as well as the frequencies of the physical signs of alcoholism, were statistically identical for both the refusal and the consenting groups who were suspected or diagnosed as having alcohol abuse, respectively.[3]

We had originally established an alcoholism prevalence rate of 34.7% among the 199 patients in our study. Adding the patients who refused study increases this prevalence figure to 37.7%. Strikingly, the number of suspected alcoholic patients jumps from 69 to 87, an increase of 26%.

Considering the two clinical services individually, 45% of those on the orthopedic service who refused inclusion in the study were suspected of alcoholism while 62% of the medical patients who refused inclusion were in this group. An adjusted estimate of the alcoholism prevalence of these respective services reveals an orthopedic surgery service prevalence of 32.7% (an increase of 1.7% over our original estimate) and a medicine service prevalence of 41.4% (a 3.9% increase).

The most striking difference in the suspected alcoholism prevalence is between those patients on the medical service who consented to the study and those who refused. Of the former group, 37.5% were diagnosed as suffering from alcoholism while 62% of the latter group were suspected of alcohol abuse on the basis of their prior histories. This difference is statistically significant (Chi Square, 1 d f, p < 0.05). No significant difference was observed among patients on the orthopedic surgery service in comparisons of the orthopedic surgery service patients and patients on the medical service.

Discussion

The results of our study suggest that alcoholism prevalence research must take into account a significant bias engendered by the investigators' request for consent for study. Our prevalence determinations for the population consenting for study were approximately 10% lower than a more realistic figure based on the inclusion of those patients who refused study. The data indicate that estimates of the total numbers of alcoholic patients seen on the two services would be increased by 20%-25% if refusal subjects were included.

We were most surprised by the high prevalence of suspected alcoholism among patients admitted to the medical service who refused to participate in the study. This rate was nearly double that seen for patients who gave consent for the survey. We have no basis from our data to suggest that these patients were more advanced in their alcoholism than were those who gave consent. The frequency with which the patients who refused study and who were suspected of alcohol abuse felt their alcohol use too private for discussion suggests that the illness had advanced to a point of increasingly lonely social adjustment. This is usually seen in the middle stages of alcoholism.

These results point up the need to incorporate systematic study of patients who refuse inclusion when designing clinical investigations of alcoholism. One approach is to conduct a chart review, as was done in this study. A second approach may lie in determining the likelihood of alcoholism based on biochemical profiles such as those developed in another aspect of this study.[4] Certainly, greater accuracy in clinical research will depend upon systematic data gathered from patients who refuse study inclusion.

REFERENCES

1. Koran, LM and Costell, RM. Early termination from group psychotherapy. Int J Group Psychotherapy, 1973; 23:346-59.

2. Kokes, RF, Fremouw, W, Strauss, JS. Lost subjects. Arch Gen Psychiatry, 1977; 34:1363-5.

3. Beresford, T, Low, D, Adduci, R, Goggans, F. The CAGE alcoholism screen questionnaire in general hospital practice. Presented at the Sixth World Congress of the International College of Psychosomatic Medicine, Montreal, Canada, September 14, 1981.

4. Beresford, T, Low, D, Hall, RCW, Adduci, R, Goggans F. A computerized diagnostic biochemical profile for the detection of alcoholism. Psychosomatics, 1982; 23: 713-20.

Group Therapy with Alcoholic Clients: A Review

Sandra C. Anderson, PhD

ABSTRACT. The literature on group therapy in alcoholism is reviewed. Topical areas include indications for group treatment, types of groups, and phases in group development and treatment. Attention is also given to therapeutic problems and methodological issues in evaluation of effectiveness. While the use of groups is popular in the treatment of alcoholism, weaknesses of evaluative studies have precluded definitive statements about their effectiveness. The incorporation of recent innovations in evaluation technology in future studies promises findings with greater reliability and validity.

Group therapy has come to be viewed by increasing numbers of authorities as the modality of choice in the treatment of alcoholism. In spite of its enthusiastic endorsement by clinicians, however, the literature on group treatment in alcoholism is relatively small, and evaluative studies tell us little about its effectiveness. The lack of adequate research in the area is, in part, reflective of unresolved issues around defining alcoholism and applying small group theory to the treatment of the alcoholic. There are many expository theories of alcoholism just as there are multiple practice theories for the use of small groups. This problem is described by Doroff[1]:

> There is a range that encompasses views of alcoholism as a medical problem, defining it as a disease entity, as well as viewing it as a mere symptomatic expression of underlying severe psychopathology. Although there are a number of technical aspects relative to the treatment of alcoholism in

Dr. Anderson is Associate Professor at the School of Social Work, Portland State University, P.O. Box 751, Portland, Oregon 97207. The author thanks Lynn E. Thompson for his valuable comments on an earlier version of this paper.

23

which rather substantial agreement exists across the technical range, there are significant differences in overall approaches to treatment which are dictated by the theoretical stance one takes. (pp. 240-241)

The purpose of this paper is to present an overview of the literature on group therapy in alcoholism. Areas covered will include indications for group treatment, types of groups, phases in group development and treatment, therapeutic problems, and evaluation of effectiveness. The writer will not attempt to analyze diverse theoretical frameworks, but will instead present an eclectic review which includes affective, cognitive, and interactional approaches. The terms "group leader" and "therapist" will be used interchangeably, and their use does not imply any particular educational background or theoretical orientation.

While there are numerous types of groups for alcoholics, this paper will focus on outpatient education and therapy groups for unrelated male and female alcoholic clients. The ways in which A.A. groups differ (in focus and approach) from many therapy groups will be addressed, but a comprehensive review of the A.A. literature is beyond the scope of this paper.

INDICATIONS FOR GROUP TREATMENT

General Issues

Competent assessment of any client involves a detailed evaluation of the problem, developmental history, and current functioning in all life areas. When developing treatment plans for alcoholic clients, the first step is to ascertain whether *any* group experience is the treatment of choice. Garvin[2] maintains that only when family treatment is considered inappropriate should the worker consider utilizing individual or group treatment. This principle may be applicable to treatment planning for alcoholics, as it has been frequently observed that excessive drinking has adaptive consequences which serve as positive reinforcers strong enough to maintain the drinking regardless of underlying causation.[3] If the assessment indicates that the drinking problem is maintained by processes operating in the family or the family opposes individual changes, family members should be involved in treatment. If these criteria are lacking or the client rejects family involvement, group therapy may be indicated.[2]

While group therapy is frequently utilized by treatment agencies for financial reasons, more significant reasons involve the nature of alcoholism itself. Lynch[4] states that groups are indicated for alcoholic clients who are lonely, moderately anxious or depressed, and who have a poor self-image or history of loss. According to Kreuger,[5] group treatment can be particularly useful for clients who are impulsive (and deny and project in individual treatment) and/or experience unsatisfying patterns of interpersonal relationship. Clients with these difficulties view confrontation in individual treatment as personal criticism and are often unable to separate transference and real aspects of the relationship. They respond more favorably to confrontation by their peers and are better able to learn new patterns of relationships in a group. One clear advantage of group treatment to the worker is the opportunity to compare actual with reported client behavior.[6]

Clinical Diagnostic Issues

In spite of these advantages, some clients are less likely to benefit from outpatient group treatment. There is some agreement that contraindications for this type of therapy include clients with the following diagnosis: organic brain syndrome, paranoid personality, schizoid personality, hypochondriacal neurosis, psychosis, and antisocial personality. In addition, clients who are suicidal, in severe external crisis, extremely narcissistic, poorly motivated, and unable to recognize important conflict areas are poor risks for outpatient group treatment.[1,7,8]

Thus, while there are some data on the most appropriate clients for group therapy in general, two significant diagnostic issues have received insufficient attention in the alcoholism literature. One is the distinction between the primary and secondary alcoholic, and the other is the distinction between the various character types within primary alcoholism.[1]

Primary vs. Secondary Alcoholism

Studies on the effectiveness of individual therapy with alcoholics indicate that treatment and outcome appear to be quite different for primary and secondary alcoholics. For example, treatment of the client with primary alcoholism (no history of major psychiatric disorder prior to the onset of alcoholism) optimally involves major focus on the drinking behavior itself, dealing appropriately with defenses, and strengthening existing coping mechanisms. Treatment of the client with secondary alcoholism (history of major psychiatric disorder prior to the onset of alcoholism) may involve the combination of tricyclic antidepressants or lithium with psychotherapy.[9] Finally, the client who is drinking excessively in response to a severe life crisis will tend to deal in treatment with the losses which precipitated the problem drinking. The client who is drinking secondary to a severe crisis or an affective disorder has a good prognosis, probably somewhat better than that of the primary alcoholic.[10] While it could be hypothesized that the diagnosis of primary or secondary alcoholism has significant implications for both content and outcome of group therapy, the issue has not been systematically studied to date.

The second diagnostic issue, the distinction between the various character types constituting primary alcoholism, has received some attention in the literature on group treatment. As mentioned, outpatient, heterogeneous group treatment is generally contraindicated for clients diagnosed as paranoid, schizoid, frankly psychotic, and antisocial. There is, however, lack of consensus on exclusion criteria when applied to groups of alcoholics. While some authors seem to adhere to the traditional criteria just mentioned, others do not. Fox,[11] for example, describes the ideal alcoholic group as "heterogeneous in terms of underlying emotional pathology which may range from near normal when abstinent, through character disorder and psychoneurosis, to borderline psychotic depressive reaction" (p. 258). This issue is clearly in need of further study, as there is much to be learned about the relationship between clinical diagnosis (and the mixture of clients with different diagnoses) and treatment effectiveness in alcoholism groups.

Demographic Variables

There is considerable agreement that alcoholics are treated most effectively in all-alcoholic groups[1,6]; findings on the combined treatment of alcohol and drug abuse clients are conflicting.[12,13] Regarding other variables in composition, Blume[6] states that "characteristics such as age, sex, education, religion, race, sexual preference, ethnic group, and social class have been mixed successfully in therapy groups for alcoholism" (pp. 66-67). Some authors, however, advocate separate groups for alcoholic women, homosexuals, and adolescents. As a general rule, the placement of one person in a group with unique characteristics should be avoided.[4,14,15]

In summary, there are several major issues involved in referral to groups and composition of groups. These include consideration of the appropriateness of family therapy and/or individual therapy, the clinical diagnosis of the client, the diagnosis of primary or secondary alcoholism, and the role of certain demographic variables. These issues have not been adequately studied and, in practice, to quote Gwinner,[16] "Criteria employed for patient selection in group therapy are poorly described and promiscuously applied" (p. 117).

TYPES OF GROUPS

There are several types of groups for alcoholics: orientation or alcohol education groups, groups of unrelated married or unmarried alcoholics, spouse groups, couples' groups, family groups, and groups of alcoholics and unrelated spouses of other alcoholics. The present discussion will focus upon the first two types of groups mentioned.

Education Groups

Orientation or alcohol education groups utilizing a lecture-discussion format are typically offered to clients during the initial intake process. Such groups serve several purposes. They provide technical information about the physiological, psychological, and social aspects of alcoholism. In addition, they introduce clients to the group experience and provide the opportunity to evaluate the helpfulness of group interaction. Finally, they provide a practical mechanism for screening clients for future treatment. During the orientation group, motivation and suitability for further group treatment can be assessed, and clients can be prepared for therapy groups.[6,17] Orientation groups usually meet for 90 minutes per week for four to six weeks.[17] Research on DUII offenders indicates that the educational model of treatment is effective with the social drinker, particularly the first offender.[18,19] The addiction of the habitual drinker, however, remains impervious to the educational model, and these clients need referral to more intensive treatment.[20]

Therapy Groups

Therapy groups composed of from six to ten clients provide members with the opportunity to learn methods of coping without alcohol. Sands and Hanson[17] point out that therapy groups allow clients to ventilate feelings, compare attitudes and behavior with others, and practice new behaviors in a safe setting. The general aim of most groups is to promote insight and/or behavioral change, i.e., to help clients understand factors that contribute to and maintain their problem drinking and to deal more effectively with them when they arise.

Whether the group is educational or therapeutic in focus, an early decision must be made about utilizing an open or closed format. This choice is more often dictated by the agency than the preferences of the leaders or clients. Closed groups (in which all clients begin treatment at the same time and remain together) have several advantages over open groups (in which new clients are added as others complete treatment or drop out). Blume[6] points out that the closed group tends to encourage more intense relationships, since members share the entire history of the group. This results in higher cohesion, as clients become attached to the group as well as to each other. In general, closed groups can be smaller in size, a factor which also tends to increase individual participation and cohesiveness.[15]

On the other hand, there are certain advantages of open groups. Since they tend to be larger, clients usually do not have to wait for entry, and the groups are not destroyed by dropouts. They also allow for more flexibility, since the length of treatment may be tailored to individual need.[6] Probably the greatest advantage is the influx of new ideas and values, sometimes resulting in greater creativity.[15] Blume[6] points out that the leader must take a more active role in open groups, as newcomers do not share the group history and often feel isolated. In both closed and open groups, the advantages of co-leadership are considerable, and co-leaders should be utilized if feasible.[4]

PHASES IN GROUP DEVELOPMENT

Formation Phase

The first (or formation) phase in group development involves the identification of goals and beginning work on tasks to achieve these goals.[15] Blume[6] stresses the importance of clearly spelling out ground rules in this phase; rules typically relate to issues of confidentiality, lateness, absence, attending meetings intoxicated, and the responsibilities of both leaders and members.

Lynch[4] recommends the use of a written contract which explicates, in addition, the following: purpose and task of the group, time and place of meetings, length and duration of sessions, expectations regarding extra-group socializing, use of tape recording, and emergency procedures. In the first session, the leader should avoid long silences, formal exercises, or allowing one member to monopolize the discussion. Group focus is on becoming acquainted, discussing feelings about being in the group, and developing the group contract.

Goal Setting. Once the ground rules have been clarified, both group and individual goals need to be derived. Therapy groups may have discrete but limited goals (e.g., abstinence or employment) or goals related to interpersonal interaction and/or character change. Both types of goals typically involve overcoming denial, increasing motivation, recognizing feelings and behavior patterns, and learning new ways to handle old problems.[6]

Blume[6] points out that the client may deny the severity of the drinking problem or the existence of any problems other than drinking. If the client is well integrated into the group, direct confrontation of denial is appropriate. Heavy-handed, relentless bombarding is antitherapeutic, however, and usually results in premature termination or passive submission to avoid future conflict. Effective confrontation enables the *client* to make connections between his/her past life and present behavior, and between drinking behavior and current life problems. While initial motivation is often based on coercion from others, self-motivation for recovery is the group goal. Periodic questioning about the motivation for recovery stresses the importance of the issue and aids in monitoring progress. Clients can learn to recognize feelings and behavior patterns by labeling here-and-now feelings in the group and by analyzing the antecedents and consequences of the behaviors they wish to change. The learning of new ways to handle old problems is enhanced by role-playing in the group and homework assignments outside the group.[6]

As mentioned, while some groups have limited goals such as abstinence, others aim at promoting significant personality change in clients. Brown and Yalom[7] and Yalom et al.[8] have written about this latter approach, called interactional group therapy. In this type of group, the goal is *not* to help members achieve or maintain sobriety, but rather to "understand and work through underlying personality conflicts that contributed to the alcohol dependency" (p. 422). Members are not encouraged to discuss alcohol explicitly but are referred to A.A. for this purpose.

Regardless of the overall group goals, it is important that each client identify personal changes he/she wishes to make. Thus, in addition to goals which apply to all alcoholic clients, specific goals need to be developed for each client in the group. Blume[6] states that typical individual goals are related to problems with responsibility, anger, depression, and fear.

Clients who assume too much responsibility for the feelings and behavior of others can be helped by the group to draw firm boundaries to their own responsibility until they are internalized. Narcissistic clients can be helped to develop a better sense of responsibility by rewarding group behavior that is helpful to others. Clients who have difficulty expressing anger can be challenged when they have good reason to be angry in the here-and-now, and clients who have difficulty controlling anger can be helped to trace the original source of anger, discharge the feeling through role-play, and learn techniques of control. Finally, clients who are depressed or fearful can be drawn out slowly to mourn losses or incrementally face their fears.[6]

In interactional group therapy, specific techniques are utilized in the formative phase to promote cohesiveness and decrease anxiety. Written agendas are prepared for each meeting, and the leader writes a detailed summary after each session and mails it to members prior to the next meeting. The summary contains a narrative process of the session as well as editorial notes on process observations, new interpretations, et cetera.[8]

Problems in the Formative Phase. In discussing common problems in this phase, Brown and Yalom[7] identify an inability to relinquish an A.A. focus and resistance to establishing norms of openness and self-exploration. In their experience, A.A. members are used to and comfortable with high support, low conflict, ritualistic meetings. When combined with drinking non-A.A. members, the group tends to divide into two subgroups and is prevented from discussing topics other than alcohol. Many A.A. members consider a drinking slip to be a disaster, feel responsible for protecting other members, and avoid any potentially conflictual material.

Brown and Yalom[7] suggest that therapists can best resolve this dilemma by directly pointing out the options available to members: They can maintain the equilibrium with comfortable but restricting defenses or risk the discomfort of change.

In addition to the reluctance to relinquish an A.A. focus, many groups resist norms of openness and self-exploration. Mullan and Sanguiliano[21] describe an early form of resistance called "quasi-group cohesion." This is manifested by a superficial camaraderie among clients intended to exclude the therapists and maintain an atmosphere of mutual support which precludes confrontation.

Ideally, the therapy group will stabilize during the formative phase and develop norms of self-disclosure and active participation of all members. This requires an active, involved leader who at the same time can encourage members to talk to each other. One-to-one helping by the leader should not be the preferred mode in the group, as it creates the expectation that all significant therapy is from the leader.[2] In spite of the best efforts of the leader in this phase, however, at times it becomes clear that the aggregate cannot and will not become a group.[15] In this case, erratic attendance and premature termination are common phenomena.

There has been considerable research on early terminators from group therapy, and there is evidence that they do not profit from their brief stay in the group. In addition, their departure often has a very negative effect on remaining group members. In groups of alcoholics, reasons for premature termination usually involve poor selection (inappropriate referral to group treatment or placement in an inappropriate group) and/or insufficient preparation for the group experience. As discussed previously, frankly psychotic and antisocial clients do not usually fare well in outpatient groups and have a high probability of terminating early without benefit. In addition, fear of intimacy is a significant reason for early departure.[22] Clients who are poorly motivated and still drinking heavily after the orientation group are poor risks, as are abstinent clients who refuse to discuss anything but alcohol and abstinence.[7]

Insufficient preparation for the group experience is believed by some to be the primary reason for premature group termination. The development of a trusting relationship between the therapist and client is the most significant aspect of preparation.[21] It is important that they meet individually prior to group entry and that the rationale for referral to group treatment be explained fully.

Group Functioning and Maintenance Phase

The working (or group functioning and maintenance) phase of development is characterized by clear norms of behavior, stable interpersonal relationship patterns, a lowering of defenses, and an increase in sharing. In the well-functioning group, leadership and status hierarchy stabilize and high cohesion develops.[15] According to Brown and Yalom,[7] certain major themes occur repetitively in this phase: Alcoholics Anonymous, alcohol, dependency, rigidity and denial, guilt and responsibility, anger, and depression.

As mentioned earlier, Alcoholics Anonymous frequently emerges as a theme in the formative phase. Techniques for handling subgrouping and resistance of A.A. members have been discussed. In the working phase, it is often necessary to stress the differences between the functions of A.A. and therapy groups. For example, while A.A. meetings are quite ritualized and focus on the achievement and maintenance of abstinence, many therapy groups focus on here-and-now interaction and the resolution of interpersonal problems. A.A. attempts to gratify dependency needs, while the therapy group does so only enough to keep the client in treatment. In essence, A.A. provides a support system which helps clients tolerate the discomfort of the therapy group. While the subject of drinking is a common bond in the formative phase, as the group progresses the differentiation between members can be increased by focusing on the various defensive functions of drinking. Denial systems and feelings of depression, as well as conflicts around dependency, responsibility, and the expression of anger can be gently recognized and confronted by a supportive group.[7]

Termination Phase

The termination phase of group treatment consists of working through the termination of the individual or group and developing a plan for follow-up. While termination is considered by many to be the most important part of therapy, there is little in the literature on either the nature or handling of group termination.

Maholick and Turner[23] state that individual termination from the group is indicated when any of the following occur: contractual ending of the treatment arrangement, client satisfaction with gains in insight and/or behavior change, unexpected reality developments, behavior consistently destructive to the group or another member, severe regression or psychotic behavior, or lack of progress in therapy. When considering termination for any of these reasons, the therapist needs to evaluate the status of the presenting problem and the client's current coping abilities. Discussion should begin 3-4 weeks before the actual termination, and should focus on which goals have and have not been achieved and feelings of loss. When the termination of a group member reactivates the leader's own conflicts about separation, the member may be pressured to delay termination or leave prematurely. This situation can be prevented by the added perspective of a co-leader.[4]

When the entire group is being terminated, denial and regression is not unusual. These phenomena are positive, as they indicate that members have formed meaningful relationships with each other and the group. It is important at this time to review the significant events of the group and assess the meaning of the group to each member.[4] All members should understand that the therapist/agency is available in the future for brief consultations and/or additional treatment if needed.

PROBLEMS IN GROUP TREATMENT

Closure and Intoxication

While some problems are common to all therapy groups, Blume[6] points out two that are specific to alcoholism treatment: closure and intoxication. Closure is an important issue in alcoholism groups since negative feelings may precipitate drinking. Thus, leaders should avoid ending sessions with members in a state of conflict. If a member is distressed toward the end of a session, he/she should be given group support and a review done of progress since entering treatment.

The problem of attending meetings intoxicated is perhaps a more common and serious one. As mentioned earlier, all groups need to establish ground rules on this issue in the formation phase. Brown and Yalom[7] allow intoxicated members to stay in the group but view their presence as a frustrating experience for the entire group. In order to derive some benefit from the episode, the drunken behavior is described in detail in the summaries distributed to all members, and the session is videotaped. These techniques are then used to process the behavior in a later session. For an excellent discussion of other techniques for dealing with the group client who drinks, the reader is referred to Vannicelli.[24] Some problems in therapy groups are not peculiar to alcoholism groups. These include issues of transference, countertransference, and resistance.

Transference

It is believed that group is the treatment of choice for some alcoholics because it dilutes the transference. Martensen-Larsen[25] attributes the lack of success in individual treatment to the inability of the alcoholic to handle the intense ambivalence in the transference. Nevertheless, transference distortions do occur in groups, although they differ in content and degree between members. Yalom[22] discusses two approaches to resolving transference in therapy groups: Consensual validation and increased leader transparency. In the first method, clients are encouraged to compare among themselves their impressions of the leader; consensus indicates accurate perceptions, while lack of consensus points to individual distortions. The second approach, increased leader transparency, involves the testing of client impressions of the therapist by gradually becoming more self-revealing in the here-and-now of the group. The issue of therapist self-disclosure is one of the most controversial ones in the field of group therapy. Some authors[26-28] contend that the person of the therapist is a potent agent for change and that knowledge about the therapist facilitates the group process. While Yalom[22] points to the effectiveness of the therapist sharing feelings in the here-and-now of the group, he notes that most therapists prefer not to share aspects of their personal lives with the group. He notes further that, at the time of termination, clients do *not* wish that the therapist had shared more of his personal problems with the group. He states that more or less unlimited transparency can result in a lack of strong leadership, losing sight of individual client needs, and neglect of the cognitive aspects of therapy. Doroff[1] goes further in hypothesizing that a "personal" approach can stimulate the fantasies of the narcissistic client that the therapist will meet all of his/her infantile needs. When these fantasies are not gratified, the resulting rage may lead to a premature termination of treatment. Martensen-Larsen[25] advocates using co-therapists to deal with transference problems in the group. This enables the client to split the transference, keeping one therapist as the benign figure and the other the object of transference anger.

Countertransference

Countertransference reactions often compromise effective group treatment. In groups of alcoholics, the unrealistic expectations of narcissistic clients often provoke very negative countertransference eactions.[29] The same reaction may be elicited from alcoholics who are borderline and/or extremely manipulative. The combined use of co-therapists, videotaping, and competent supervision can aid in the resolution of these problems.

Resistance

As in individual treatment, clients in groups continually resist treatment by defense mechanisms. According to Fox,[11] the most common defenses in alcoholism groups are regression, denial, introjection, projection, and rationalization. She believes that the basic resistance is to *permanent sobriety* and to the loss of what alcohol does for the client.[30]

Doroff[1] points out that acting-out as the basic resistance is the central problem in the treatment of all alcoholic clients. Acting-out can take many forms in group treatment, ranging from in-group behaviors such as scapegoating, dominating the session, and prolonged storytelling, to serious nongroup behaviors such as romantic attachments with other clients and getting arrested. Repeated drinking episodes are a common form of acting-out, sometimes followed by requests for individual appointments. Blume[6] suggests that this be handled by exploring the reasons for the request and reassuring the client that the matter is appropriate for discussion in the group.

In summary, some problems in therapy groups, such as closure and intoxication, are specific to groups of alcoholics. Problems emanating from transference and countertransference reactions and resistance, however, are characteristic of all therapy groups. While these problems may be diluted in a group, they are nevertheless always present to some degree and deserve careful attention as part of the interactional process.

EVALUATION OF EFFECTIVENESS

Evaluation of Individual Change in Groups

Garvin[2] discusses several specific measurement techniques for evaluating individual change in a small group: Behavioral counts, goal attainment scaling, self-ratings on emotional scales, and psychological instruments. The use of behavioral counts involves tabulating the number of times a member engages in a desired act such as completing homework assignments, drinking in a controlled manner, or seeking out nondrinking friends. Goal attainment scaling involves the development of individual goals for each client and evaluating each goal on a five-level scale ranging from the most favorable to the most unfavorable outcome. This method is time-consuming, but underscores the importance of individualized treatment planning within the group. Finally, self-ratings on emotional states and standardized psychological instruments are short and easy to administer and score, making them appropriate for periodic use throughout treatment. All of these approaches are feasible for use in single system evaluation of alcoholism groups, and can be utilized as part of an overall plan for evaluating treatment effectiveness of a particular program or agency. While methods of evaluating group *process* are available,[2] outcome data specific to alcoholism groups are lacking.

Methodological Issues

There have been numerous reviews of the methodological problems encountered in alcoholism treatment evaluation. These include failure to assign subjects randomly to treatment conditions, use of retrospective as opposed to planned treatment outcome studies, use of insensitive measures of treatment outcome, failure to assess the reliability and validity of measures, and poor follow up techniques.[31,32] These methodological problems are not idiosyncratic to alcoholism treatment evaluation, and are pervasive in studies of both individual and group treatment.

Individual clinical accounts on the effectiveness of group therapy range from dismal to glowing. For example, one former client in a therapy group concluded that "only a deep sense of frustration at the thought that so many alcoholics are looking for help would make me suggest group-therapy"[33] (p. 77). On the other hand,

Brown and Yalom[7] found that, at 12 months, alcoholic clients in interactional group therapy had outcomes equivalent in every way to nonalcoholic neurotic clients in similar types of groups.

Parloff[34] conducted an extensive review of group therapy outcome research, and concluded that "studies with drug addicts and alcoholics tell us surprisingly little about the pragmatic efficacy of group psychotherapy with addictive disorders" (p. 310). Again, it is clear that most studies in this area have methodological weaknesses common throughout the evaluation literature in the behavioral and social sciences. There are, however, several issues unique to the evaluation of alcoholism treatment. These include abstinence as a criterion of success, the validity and reliability of self-reports by alcoholics, and the difficulty of locating alcoholics for follow up.

Abstinence as a Criterion for Success. The use of abstinence as a criterion of success has been questioned by many authorities, and there is considerable agreement that success must be assessed in terms of multiple outcome variables. The current trend in evaluation research is to examine broader dimensions of outcome which include total life adjustment and adaptation.[35] It could be argued that abstinence is just the beginning of positive changes attainable through group therapy. One recent study[36] found that alcoholic patients wanted much more from treatment than simply ending their dependence on alcohol; they also wanted psychological treatment, school and job counseling, and recreational guidance.

Validity and Reliability of Self-Reports. Alcohol treatment evaluation relies heavily on self-reports of alcoholics in spite of a widespread belief that alcoholics are prone to excessive denial and even intentional lying. This belief may be fallacious, as Sobell and Sobell[37] found that not only were self-reports of alcoholics valid and reliable, but also discovered that court-mandated clients gave self-reports as valid as those of clients who voluntarily entered treatment. Caddy[38] suggests that deception can be minimized if data collection is an integral part of therapy and follow up, and if the client sees the strategies used to collect information as relevant to his or her recovery.

Difficulty of Locating Alcoholics for Follow-Up. The majority of evaluative studies have very low follow-up rates, and this clearly biases the findings of even well-designed studies. While high client loss at follow up is usually attributed to client characteristics (e.g., high mobility or reluctance to disclose treatment failure), most reviewers agree that it is more appropriately related to lack of funds and personnel, faulty techniques, and the attitude that alcoholics are hard to locate.[39] Caddy[38] believes that client loss can be virtually eliminated if evaluation is integrated into the service delivery system, collateral sources are fully utilized in tracking clients, and if there are frequent and continued contacts with clients.

In summary, methodological weaknesses of evaluative studies of group treatment have precluded definitive statements about the effectiveness of this modality. There is a critical need for well-designed prospective studies. Recent innovations in evaluation technology are promising, and the incorporation of research into ongoing treatment activities will undoubtedly result in more successful studies in the future.

CONCLUSIONS

Group therapy is viewed by many as the modality of choice in the treatment of alcoholism. While groups are used extensively in alcoholism programs, the professional literature in the area is small, and there is little empirical research on effectiveness relative to other modalities. This state of affairs is not peculiar to group treatment of alcoholism. As stated by Luft[40]:

> There is ample precedent in the history of science for unevenness in the development of theory and application. Man could sail long before he understood the aerodynamics of hull and wing. Face-to-face interaction has always existed, but it will be a long time before we really understand how interaction works. The order is a large one: to understand man in relation to man. If our current knowledge is limited, spotty, contradictory, and foolish, that at least tells us where we are, and everyone is invited to improve on it. (p. 3)

REFERENCES

1. Doroff D. Group psychotherapy in alcoholism. In: Kissin B, Begleiter H, eds. The biology of alcoholism, Vol. 5. Treatment and rehabilitation of the chronic alcoholic. New York: Plenum, 1977.

2. Garvin C. Contemporary group work. New Jersey: Prentice-Hall, Inc., 1981.

3. Davis D, Berenson D, Steinglass P, Davis S. The adaptive consequences of drinking. Psychiatry. 1974; 37:209-15.

4. Lynch M. Starting a counseling group. In: Group skills for alcoholism counselors: Readings (Publication No. 80-992). Arlington, Virginia: National Center for Alcohol Education, 1980.

5. Kreuger D. Clinical considerations in the prescription of group, brief, long-term, and couples psychotherapy. Psychiatr Q. 1979; 51:92-105.

6. Blume S. Group psychotherapy in the treatment of alcoholism. In: Zimberg S, Wallace J, Blume S, eds. Practical approaches to alcoholism psychotherapy. New York: Plenum, 1978.

7. Brown S, Yalom I. Interactional group therapy with alcoholics. J Stud Alcohol. 1977; 38:426-56.

8. Yalom I, Block S, Bond G, Zimmerman E, Qualls B. Alcoholics in interactional group therapy. Arch Gen Psychiatry. 1978; 35:419-25.

9. Hollister L. Clinical uses of psychotherapeutic drugs. Springfield, Illinois: Charles C Thomas, 1973.

10. Schuckit M, Winokur G. A short-term followup of women alcoholics. Dis Nerv Syst. 1972; 33:672-8.

11. Fox R. Modifications of group psychotherapy for alcoholics. Am J Orthopsychiatry. 1965; 35:258-9.

12. Pinney E, Schimizzi G, Johnson N. Group psychotherapy for substance abuse patients: development of a technique. Int J Addict. 1979; 14:437-43.

13. Cole S, Lehman W, Cole E. Combined treatment for alcohol and drug abuse clients: inpatient versus outpatient treatment settings. Fort Worth, Texas: Institute of Behavioral Research, Texas Christian University, 1978.

14. Davis L. Racial composition of groups. Soc Work. 1979; 24:208-13.

15. Hartford M. Groups in social work. New York: Columbia University Press, 1972.

16. Gwinner P. Treatment approaches. In: Grant M, Gwinner P, eds. Alcoholism in perspective. Baltimore: University Park Press, 1979.

17. Sands P, Hanson P. Psychotherapeutic groups for alcoholics and relatives in an outpatient setting. Int J Group Psychother. 1971; 21:23-33.

18. Eddy J. A DWI educational program. J Drug Educ. 1976; 6:137-40.

19. McGuire F. The effectiveness of a treatment program for the alcohol involved driver. Am J Drug Alcohol Abuse. 1978; 5:517-25.

20. Kern J, Schmelter W, Paul S. Drinking drivers who complete and drop out of an alcohol education program. J Stud Alcohol. 1977; 38:89-95.

21. Mullan H, Sanguiliano I. Alcoholism: Group psychotherapy and rehabilitation. Springfield, Illinois: Charles C Thomas, 1966.

22. Yalom I. The theory and practice of group psychotherapy. New York: Basic Books, Inc., 1975.

23. Maholick L, Turner D. Termination: That difficult farewell. Am J Psychother. 1979; 33:583-91.

24. Vannicelli M. Issues in group counseling with alcoholic clients. In: Group skills for alcoholism counselors: Readings (Publication No. 80-992). Arlington, Virginia: National Center for Alcohol Education, 1980.

25. Martensen-Larsen O. Group psychotherapy with alcoholics in private practice. Int J Group Psychother. 1956; 6:28-37.

26. Apter N. Breaking the rules. In: Gunderson J, Mosher L, eds. Psychotherapy of schizophrenia. New York: Jason Aronson, 1975.

27. Aronson G. Crucial aspects of therapeutic intervention. In: Gunderson J, Mosher, L, eds. Psychotherapy of schizophrenia. New York: Jason Aronson, 1975.

28. Cadogan D. Marital group therapy in alcoholism treatment. In: Kaufman E, Kaufmann P, eds. Family therapy of drug and alcohol abuse. New York: Gardner Press, 1979.

29. Giovacchinni P. Technical difficulties in treating some characterological disorders: Counter transference problems. Int J Psychoanal Psychother. 1972; 1:112-28.

30. Fox R. Group psychotherapy with alcoholics. Int J Group Psychother. 1962; 12: 56-63.

31. Maistro S, Cooper A. A historical perspective on alcohol and drug treatment outcome research. In: Sobell L, Sobell M, Ward E, eds. Evaluating alcohol and drug abuse treatment effectiveness: recent advances. New York: Pergamon Press, 1980.

32. Voegtlin W, Lemere F. Treatment of alcohol addiction: a review of the literature. Q J Stud Alcohol. 1942; 2:717-803.

33. Macphail D. Personal experience of group-therapy for alcoholism: a critical examination. Lancet. 1965; 2:75-7.

34. Parloff M, Dies R. Group psychotherapy outcome research. Int J Group Psychother. 1977; 27:281-319.

35. Belasco J. The criterion question revisited. Br J Addict. 1971; 66:39-44.

36. Duvall J, Ochs B, Lorei T, Baker S. Treatment goals of alcohol-dependent and drug-dependent patients. Int J Addict. 1980; 15:419-25.

37. Sobell L, Sobell M. Validity of self-reports in three populations of alcoholics. J Consult Clin Psychol. 1978; 46:901-7.

38. Caddy G. Problems in conducting alcohol treatment outcome studies: a review. In: Sobell L, Sobell M, Ward E, eds. Evaluating alcohol and drug abuse treatment effectiveness: recent advances. New York: Pergamon Press, 1980.

39. Hill M, Blane H. Evaluation of psychotherapy with alcoholics: a critical review. Q J Stud Alcohol. 1967; 28:76-104.

40. Luft J. Of human interaction. Palo Alto, California: National Press Books, 1969.

General Indicators
of Alcohol-Related Mortality
for United States Counties

Robert A. Wilson
Edward C. Ratledge
Henry J. Malin

ABSTRACT. Relationships among several alcohol-related mortality measures for continental United States counties (1975-1977) are analyzed. Three indices are developed through factor analysis: a single-factor index which combines all of the mortality indicators, a composite index which reflects mainly a combination alcohol-related health problems and homicide, and an index which reflects a combination of alcohol-related accidents and suicide. Correlational analysis confirms that the explanatory power of the combined indices is considerably greater than the individual mortality variables.

Alcoholism and alcohol problems appear increasingly to encompass a wider spectrum of medical and social ills. Originally limited to a narrowly defined category of alcohol addicts, the alcohol problem is now generally acknowledged to include drinking drivers, weekend drunks, pregnant drinkers, and a variety of prealcoholics who manifest a high risk of becoming alcoholics.[1] Faced with developing effective programming, administrators and planners must assess the needs of small areas for competing treatment and prevention programs in both the long and short term. Besides

---

Robert A. Wilson and Edward C. Ratledge are affiliated with the College of Urban Affairs and Public Policy, University of Delaware, Newark, DE 19711. Henry J. Malin is with the National Institute on Alcohol Abuse and Alcoholism, P. O. Box 1156, Rockville, MD 20850.

This research was conducted under sponsorship of the Alcohol Epidemiologic Data System (AEDS) operated by the General Electric Company under contract to the National Institute on Alcohol Abuse and Alcoholism (NIAAA). We thank Neil Munch of General Electric and Dr. Charles Kaelber of NIAAA for their aid and encouragement in this work.

responding to the immediate treatment needs of an ill population, the emergent and hidden needs of other high risk populations which can benefit from primary and secondary prevention must be considered. Prevalence indicators which monitor a wide spectrum of alcohol problems are required. However, the effectiveness of any single or summary indicator has yet to be adequately demonstrated. This research tests the feasibility of combining a variety of alcohol-related mortality measures into several summary indices.

Indicators of Alcohol Problem Prevalence

In alcohol epidemiology, mortality rates suggest, at minimum, that a problem once existed. Numerous techniques have evolved which purport to estimate the number of living alcoholics from the number of their deceased counterparts.[2,3] Prevalence estimates may be based on a number of different "alcohol-related" causes of death, on household surveys of "problem drinkers," alcoholic beverage sales, and on treatment program admissions and discharges. Usually, a numerical estimate of the number or rate of alcoholics or problem drinkers residing in an area is produced. When several estimating techniques are employed, however, the results may vary substantially.[4] If two different prevalence estimating methodologies reveal a systematic relationship across geographic areas, then either indicator (with a linear adjustment) can be used as a surrogate for the other. In contrast, if the two indicators do not vary systematically across areas, then it is likely that the two methods are measuring different pathologies which may be prevalent in two different populations at risk.

In sum, most alcoholism prevalence estimates for small areas employ a very general definition of the alcohol problems which are being measured. They assume that cirrhosis mortality signifies the same prevalence pool as does heavy drinking, problem drinking, or admission to an alcohol treatment program. In fact, each of these indicators may be related to a completely different subpopulation. Analysis of the covariation of the various indicators over different population groups is one way of exploring this issue. The reduction of the large number of candidate prevalence measures to a smaller array of statistically independent summary indicators is the fundamental task in the development of meaningful alcohol problem risk estimations.

The Development of County-Level Alcohol Problem Indicators

This article summarizes the results of an analysis of alcohol problem indicators for the continental United States counties for the years 1975-1977. Because the county is frequently the basic unit for planning and administering treatment and prevention programs, it is important to gauge the prevalence of a variety of different kinds of alcohol problems at this level of geographic analysis.[5,6] It is also important to determine whether counties which manifest high levels of one alcohol problem, e.g., cirrhosis mortality, typically manifest high levels of other alcohol-related problems, e.g., automobile fatalities. If this pattern of covariation is evident, the construction of a combined index based on a common variance is justified. If the various problem indicators do not covary across counties, then each problem indicator should be considered separately. In short, the underlying issue is whether different alcohol problems of small areas are manifest in a single population at risk, or several subpopulations.

Method

The indicators employed in this analysis consist of mortality rates for the years 1975-1977 (Table 1). Complete data for a total of 3,103 counties of the continental United States are employed.* Seven alcohol-related causes of death are analyzed: cirrhosis, alcoholism, alcohol psychosis, alcohol poisoning, suicide, homicide, and fatal automobile accidents.

The cirrhosis rates employed include all cirrhosis deaths for the three-year period studied—not only those with alcohol mention, but also those without.** Suicide, homicide, and fatal automobile accidents are also included in the variable set. Although many deaths attributed to these causes are not directly related to alcohol, other studies have confirmed consistently that alcohol is involved in disproportionate number.[7] Moreover, because the county, rather

---

*The five New York boroughs are combined into a single observation because county of residence classification for mortality data were not included at the borough level. Six counties of Virginia were excluded from the analysis because demographic base information was unavailable in the form required.

**Because cirrhosis with alcohol-mention (571.1) appears to be verified and recorded differently across jurisdictions, the more inclusive measure (all cirrhosis deaths—571) appears to be the more reliable indicator of alcohol-related mortality.

TABLE 1

DATA BASE EMPLOYED FOR CONSTRUCTION OF
COUNTY LEVEL ALCOHOL PROBLEM INDICES *

		Mean	Standard Deviation
1.	Cirrhosis Mortality (ICDA 571 for 1975, 1976, and 1977, per 100,000 population aged 15-74 years) SOURCE: National Center for Health Statistics (NCHS)	15.29	11.86
2.	Alcoholism Mortality (ICDA 303 for 1975, 1976, and 1977, per 100,000 population aged 15-74 years SOURCE: NCHS	3.24	4.83
3.	Alcohol Psychosis Mortality (ICDS 291 for 1975, 1976, and 1977, per 100,000 population aged 15-74 years) SOURCE: NCHS	.33	1.28
4.	Alcohol Poisoning Mortality (ICDA 860 for 1976, 1976, and 1977, per 100,000 population aged 15-74 years) SOURCE: NCHS	.28	1.13
5.	Suicide Mortality (ICDA 955 for 1975, 1976, and 1977, per 100,000 population aged 15-74 years) SOURCE: NCHS	17.29	10.26
6.	Homicides (ICDA 960 for 1975, 1976 1977, per 100,000 population aged 15-74 years) SOURCE: NCHS	10.14	11.21
7.	Fatal Accidents (ICDA 810-811, Motor Vehicle, 820-823, Other Fatal Automobile Accidents, Non-Traffic for 1975, 1976, and 1977, per 100,000 population aged 15-74 years) SOURCE: NCHS	44.80	36.52

*Estimations of 1975 County population aged 15 and above were provided by the National Cancer Institute.

N = 3,103 Counties

than the individual, is the unit of analysis in this study, the relationship between the traditional alcohol problem indicators and other social pathology indicators becomes of prime importance in program planning. The resulting set of variables consists of a limited set of mortality measures for which full coverage of United States counties is available. The decision to use these variables was based on their statistical summary capacity and their availability over counties throughout the continental United States. A three-year average (1975-1977) is employed in the analysis.

Even with the limited set of summary alcohol problem indicators employed, a great deal of redundancy is possible. Several variables may, in fact, indicate the same underlying alcohol problem in a county. The main question centers around the utility of a single summary index which is associated with all of the alcohol indicators, as compared to several indices which are associated with different types of alcohol-related mortality. If the mortality indicators covary systematically across counties, then the use of a single index is justified. If, however, the indicators do not reveal this covariation, then the advisability of different indicators for different alcohol problems is warranted. Factor analysis is used as a data reduction procedure—to identify both a single composite indicator and two separate indicators, derived from the same set of alcohol-related mortality data.†

Results

When the variables are forced into a single factor solution, all of the variables show moderate loadings (correlations with a common underlying factor—Table 2). The two highest factor loadings are

TABLE 2

FACTOR LOADINGS FOR SINGLE FACTOR
ALCOHOL PROBLEM INDEX, UNITED STATES COUNTIES 1975–1977*

	Composite Alcohol Problem Index	
Variable	Loading	Communality
Cirrhosis Mortality	.454	.206
Alcohol Psychosis Mortality	.149	.022
Alcoholism Mortality	.553	.305
Alcohol Poisoning Mortality	.220	.048
Suicide	.346	.120
Homicide	.388	.150
Fatal Accidents	.308	.095

Eigenvalue is .946.

Total Variance Explained: 13.54 percent

* Complete data from all counties were employed;
therefore no adjustments for missing data were required.

N = 3,103

---

†The Statistical Package for the Social Sciences (Version H, level 7.2) was employed.

cirrhosis mortality and alcoholism mortality (also reflected in their communality, which shows a variable's relative contribution to the variation in the total dependent variable set). The single factor solution confirms the feasibility of combining all of the alcohol problem variables into a Composite Alcohol Problem Index. The second factor analysis explores whether two indices which are statistically independent can be derived. In the single factor solution (Table 2) three variables: alcohol psychosis, alcohol poisoning, and fatal accidents registered a low degree of communality, signifying that they reflect dimensions of alcohol problems other than those summarized by the single-factor model. Fatal accidents, in particular, reflect another (statistically independent) dimension of county alcohol problems. In the two-factor solution, a varimax rotation is employed, resulting in two factors which are relatively statistically independent of each other (Table 3). In the first factor (1) the highest loadings are registered by cirrhosis, alcoholism, alcohol poisoning, and homicide. In this factor the traditional alcohol mortality variables (cirrhosis and alcoholism) along with homicide, vary together across counties. In contrast, the second factor

TABLE 3

FACTOR LOADINGS, TWO-FACTOR VARIMAX SOLUTION,
ALCOHOL PROBLEM INDICATORS, UNITED STATES COUNTIES, 1975–1977

Variable	Chronic Health Problems Factor 1	Alcohol Casualties Factor 2	Communality
Cirrhosis Mortality	.382	.248	.208
Alcohol Psychosis Mortality	.132	.076	.023
Alcoholism Mortality	.404	.358	.291
Alcohol Poisoning Mortality	.377	-.053	.145
Suicide	.167	.333	.139
Homicide	.351	.192	.160
Fatal Automobile Accidents	.019	.498	.249
Eigenvalue	.970	.245	
Percentage of Variance Explained (rotated matrix):	8.84	8.84	

N = 3,103

(2) loads most highly on alcoholism, suicide, and fatal accidents. In sum, the first factor (1) appears to signify chronic health problems which are alcohol-related. The second appears to reflect alcohol-related casualties.

Another way of evaluating the feasibility of employing individual alcohol problem variables or summary indices is to compare the intercorrelations of the total variable set to gauge the capacity of each variable to predict other alcohol indicators in the data set (including the one- and two-factor indices). The intercorrelations of the seven alcohol problem variables reveal a uniformly low to moderate set of associations (Table 4). No single variable among the basic seven is a strong predictor of any of the others. Examining the correlations of the component variables (1-7) with the composite factors scores (8), however, reveals a uniformly moderate to high set of correlations. This result confirms both the comprehensive scope and predictive power of the single factor indicator.

The Chronic Health and Alcohol Casualties indices (9 and 10), as expected, also reveal a different pattern of association with the individual component variables. The two factor indices have the capacity to discriminate between types of county mortality patterns which covary on two distinctively different variable sets. The Chronic Health Factor (1) exhibits a strong covariation among cirrhosis, alcoholism, and homicide. In contrast, the second (Alcohol Casualties) shows a strong covariation among alcoholism, suicide, and fatal accidents.

Discussion

Traditional analysis of alcohol-related mortality has focused principally on single causes of death. However, when analyzing smaller geographic areas, such as counties, the number of deaths associated with any one cause is frequently too small to allow meaningful and reliable interpretation. Combining several alcohol-related causes of mortality into summary indicators offers an alternative to the use of purely synthetic estimates. This paper explores the feasibility of several combinations of alcohol-related causes of death into summary measures for counties, thereby compensating for the absence of large numbers of single causes.

Factor analysis is employed as a data reduction technique and to assess the feasibility of combining the number of alcohol-related causes of death into summary indices. The patterns which emerge

TABLE 4

PRODUCT-MOMENT CORRELATIONS AMONG ALCOHOL MORTALITY RATES UNITED STATES
COUNTIES, 1975-1977*

	(1) Cirrhosis Mortality	(2) Alcohol Psychosis Mortality	(3) Alcoholism Mortality	(4) Alcohol Poisoning Mortality	(5) Suicide	(6) Homicide
(1) Cirrhosis Mortality	1.000	.108	.227	.116	.187	.184
(2) Alcohol Psychosis Mortality	.108	1.000	.076	.054	-.004	.039
(3) Alcoholism Mortality	.227	.076	1.000	.140	.185	.223
(4) Alcohol Poisoning Mortality	.116	.054	.140	1.000	.050	.126
(5) Suicide	.187	-.004	.185	.050	1.000	.095
(6) Homicide	.184	-.039	.223	.126	.095	1.000
(7) Fatal Accidents	.107	.068	.191	-.022	.169	.115
(8) Single Factor Variables 1-7	.616	.202	.750	.298	.470	.525
(9) Factor 1, 2 Factor Sol. Variables 1-7	.608	.210	.643	.600	.265	.557
(10) Factor 2, 2 Factor Sol. Variables 1-7	.396	.121	.571	-.084	.531	.307

* All correlations are significant at the .01 level (N = 3,103 counties).

TABLE 4

PRODUCT-MOMENT CORRELATIONS AMONG ALCOHOL MORATLITY RATES
UNITED STATES COUNTIES, 1975-1977*
CONT'D

	(7) Fatal Accidents	(8) Composite Factor	(9) Chronic Health Factor (1)	(10) Alcohol Casualty Factor (2)
(1) Cirrhosis Mortality	.107	.616	.608	.396
(2) Alcohol Psychosis Mortality	.068	.202	.210	.121
(3) Alcoholism Mortality	.191	.750	.643	.571
(4) Alcohol Poisoning Mortality	-.022	.298	.600	-.084
(5) Suicide	.169	.470	.265	.531
(6) Homicide	.115	.525	.557	.307
(7) Fatal Accidents	1.000	.418	.030	.795
(8) Single Factor Variables 1-7	.418	1.000	---	---
(9) Factor 1, 2 Factor Sol. Variables 1-7	.030	---	1.000	---
(10) Factor 2 2 Factor Sol. Variables 1-7	.795	---	---	1.000

* All correlations are significant at the .01 level (N = 3,103 counties).

show that it is possible (from a statistical point of view) to com-
bine the causes of death into a single summary index and into a
two-factor index.

The composite factor does indeed portray an average alcohol-
related mortality risk for counties, but includes a number of mortality measures which do not typically covary over counties. The
Chronic Health and Alcohol Casualty Factors display a more inter-
pretable pattern for the typical county. In this two-factor model,
instead of combining causes of death which may be unrelated to a
common prevalence pool, separate indicators are developed for
clusters of causes of deaths which covary across counties. The first
factor of the two-factor analysis (Chronic Health) loads most
highly on cirrhosis, alcoholism, and homicide. The second factor
(Alcohol Casualties), in contrast, loads most highly on alcoholism,
suicide, and fatal automobile accidents. The statistical indepen-
dence of these two factors suggests that these two types of mortality may occur in two different types of populations at risk. The
Chronic Health Factor appears to be indicative of problems which
are associated with the need for alcoholism treatment programs
(e.g., detoxification, residential, and outpatient treatment). In contrast, the Alcohol Casualty Factor suggests a potential need for
prevention programs and problem-drinking driver programs.
Clearly, the two-factor analysis is more useful to the planner who
must consider the relative needs for different treatment and prevention resources. The single-factor model, however, suggests a summary measure of general alcohol mortality risk which is more useful in making a case to the public or to state legislatures which are
concerned with the relative level of the overall alcohol problem
across counties.

An example of the use of the indices and their component parts
may be found in the consideration of the three counties of the State
of Delaware (Table 5). New Castle County reveals the highest
mortality rates for almost all of the component variables. Sussex
County is next highest and Kent County is lowest: On the single
factor scores New Castle County and Sussex County rank 407 and
574 in the national sample of 3,103 counties. The Chronic Health
Factor scores of the two counties reflect the slightly higher rates of
cirrhosis and alcoholism in New Castle County. However, the relative ranking of the two counties on the Alcohol Casualty Factor
reverse. Sussex County has the higher rate on automobile fatalities, New Castle the lower. The combined indicators clearly signal

TABLE 5

ALCOHOL PROBLEM INDICATORS * FOR THREE COUNTIES OF THE STATE OF DELAWARE

	County		
	Kent	New Castle	Sussex
Cirrhosis Mortality	17.5	26.2	24.5
Alcohol Pscychosis Mortality	0.0	0.1	0.5
Alcoholism Mortality	2.1	7.8	4.8
Alcohol Poisoning Mortality	0.0	0.1	0.0
Fatal Highway Accident Mortality	23.8	27.8	53.2
Suicide Mortality	12.7	17.1	17.0
Homicide Mortality	10.6	12.6	17.0
Single Factor Rank-Nationwide **	1804/3103	507/3103	574/3103
Chronic Health Factor Rank- ** Nationwide	1370/3103	419/3103	623/3103
Alcohol Casualty Factor Score- Nationwide	2270/3103	886/3103	579/3103

---

*Per 100,000 population, age 15-74 years

** Rankings are relative to the highest of the 3103 US counties on each indicator score. For example, Kent County is 1804 on the Single Factor Score, indicating that 1803 of the 3103 counties had higher (more severe) levels of alcohol problems.

programming priorities which are less discernible in the individual indicators. As a result, program priorities and policy choices are made more clear.

While it is beyond the scope of this paper to analyze the demographic structure of counties which register varying patterns on the three indices, past research at the county level has shown the importance of demographics in explaining such patterns.[6] The analysis of the county demographic patterns associated with the three summary indices promises to yield valuable insights into the varying community structures which are associated with the different clusterings of alcohol-related mortality.

REFERENCES

1. U.S. Department of Health, Education, and Welfare. Third Special Report to U.S. Congress on alcohol and health, technical support document. Washington, DC: U.S. Government Printing Office, 1978.

2. Jellinek EM. The estimate of the number of alcoholics in the U.S.A. for 1949 in light of the sixth revision of International Lists of Causes of Death. Q. J. Stud. Alcohol, 1952; 13:215-8.

3. Creative Socio-Medics Corporation. Develop improved estimates of the current prevalence of alcohol abuse and alcoholism. Final report, prepared for the National Institute on Alcohol Abuse and Alcoholism. Arlington, VA, 1977.

4. U.S. Department of Health and Human Services. Fourth Special Report to U.S. Congress on Alcohol and Health. Washington, DC: U.S. Government Printing Office, 1980.

5. Cleary PD. A standardized estimator of the prevalence of alcoholism based on mortality data. Q. J. Stud. Alcohol, 40:408-18.

6. Donnely PG. Alcohol problems and sales in the counties of Pennsylvania. Q. J. Stud. Alcohol, 1978; 39:848-51.

7. Day N. Alcohol and mortality. In: Vital statistics of the United States, Vol. III. Washington, DC: U.S. Government Printing Office, 1975.

Marijuana Use in Alcoholism: Demographic Characteristics and Effects on Therapy

David Benzer, DO
Paul Cushman, Jr., MD

ABSTRACT. Six hundred fifty patients entering treatment for drug and alcohol abuse at De Paul Hospital over a 4-month period in 1981 received a urine drug screen for cannabinoids upon admission. A random selection of 170 had 154 with alcoholism or cannabis dependency. Forty-seven (30.5%) of these had a positive urine screen of THC upon admission. Of these 47, 37 (79%) admitted recent use of marijuana when questioned during their intake interview just prior to urine screening. Only 10 (21%) denied recent cannabis use. Therefore, there was a minimal underreporting of recent cannabis use by patients entering a drug and alcohol treatment center. Also, recent cannabis use had little impact on successful initial engagement of patients into treatment. Therefore, it would appear that routine urine screening of THC in patients entering treatment is not necessary if a thorough history of drug use is obtained by competent interviewers.

I. Introduction

Marijuana (cannabis) has become increasingly popular as a mood altering drug and extensive research efforts in recent years have been devoted to the pharmacological, epidemiological, and health consequences of its use.[1-4] Most incidence and prevalence data are based on self-reports, and such data may lack precision in view of the unreliability of human recall. Also, the variability of

The authors are affiliated with the De Paul Rehabilitation Hospital. Direct reprint requests to: David Benzer, DO, De Paul Hospital, 4143 South 13th Street, Milwaukee, WI 53221.

The authors wish to gratefully acknowledge the assistance of Mr. William Zupek in data processing, and Shirley Larson in manuscript preparation.

interviewers employed to elicit drug-use histories may adversely affect the validity and reliability of self-reports. There is always the possibility that underreporting, or even denial as with alcohol abusers, may occur when attempts are made to relate cannabis to behavior, health, and psychological states.

It is increasingly apparent that drug abusers infrequently confine themselves to only one class of drugs. For example, most alcoholics in treatment are also addicted to cigarette smoke and many use excessive stimulants or sedatives.[5] Opioid addicts in treatment usually are tobacco smokers, and many are alcohol and/or other drug abusers.[6] It was, therefore, of interest to study the relationships between the reporting of cannabis use by history and the urinary detection of cannabinoids in the intake urines in a population of patients entering an alcoholism treatment center. In addition to prevalence information of cannabis use, it was hoped to compare the short-term treatment outcomes of those alcoholics whose urines, histories, or both denoted recent cannabis use from noncannabis users, i.e., those who denied recent cannabis use and lacked detectable cannabinoids in their intake urines.

II. Patients and Methods

All patients entering De Paul Rehabilitation Hospital during June-September 1981 were studied. The sample included 650 persons with alcohol and/or other drug abuse problems seeking direct hospital admission (about 400) or direct outpatient care (about 250) in Milwaukee, Wisconsin.

De Paul Rehabilitation Hospital offers group-supported, abstinence-oriented outpatient treatment to patients, scheduled to last at least six months with at least weekly attendance required. The inpatient program uses similar goals and lasts 30 days. In 1981, 1550 patients admitted to the inpatient program stayed an average of 22.4 days. All patients had a urinary drug screen on admission, which included a cannabinoid determination as well as alcohol, nicotine, stimulants, opioids, and sedatives. A complete physical examination; other laboratory work; and an extensive medical, drug, alcohol, and psychosocial history were completed on admission.

The cannabinoids were detected by the EMIT System[7] which was stated by the manufacturer to be specific and sensitive for Δ^9 Tetrahydrocannabinol and its metabolites at urinary concentrations as low as 50 ng/ml. Opioids, stimulants, alcohol, nicotine, sedatives, and hypnotics were screened by thin layer paper chromatography.

A retrospective chart review of 170 persons randomly selected from the sample group of 650 was performed. One hundred and fifty-four patients had a DMS-III diagnosis of alcoholism, or cannabis dependency; 16 other patients had a screen showing a drug dependency other than alcohol or cannabis and were dropped from the study group. Of the 154 patients, 56% were treated on an inpatient basis, while 44% were seen in the Outpatient Clinic. They were 70% male with a mean age of 32.31 yrs (range 13-76). The majority were Caucasian (83%), employed (55%), high school graduates (70%). Thus, they were largely white, economically stable, middle-class persons. From the medical point of view they were usually judged to be well, except for their drug/alcohol abuse. Few had such gross distortion of health as pancreatitis, cirrhosis, peripheral neuropathies or dementias. All were ambulatory and few would fit the skid row type of stereotypic alcoholic.

III. Results

Marijuana detection in the intake urines is listed in Table I. Overall, 47 patients (30.5%) had a positive urine drug screen for cannabis upon admission. As expected, there were greater numbers of positives in the younger age groups (Table II). Also overrepresented were black and single persons. Similarly, the histories of marijuana use was inversely related to age in the ever-used, daily-use, and recent-use (within the past 30 days) categories.

There was a close relationship between admitted recent use (within 30 days) and the urinary detections. Of the 47 patients with positive urine THC screens, 37 (79%) admitted recent use of marijuana. Only 10 (21%) patients with positive urine THC screens denied recent use. Therefore, there was little systematic underreporting of recent cannabis use by these patients at the time of their intake interview, contrary to expectation.

The relationship between marijuana use and the rate of engagement of alcoholic patients into initial treatment process is found in Table III. Since significant changes in behavior or drug abuse are unlikely after only a short time in treatment, it was of interest to evaluate the apparent presence or absence of cannabis use as a factor influencing initial treatment process. Initial treatment engage-

TABLE I

THC Use by Alcoholic Patients Entering Treatment

(n=154)

THC USE	YES	NO
POSITIVE URINE SCREEN	47 (31%)	107 (69%)
EVER USED	88 (57%)	66 (43%)
RECENT USE (within 30 days)	49 (32%)	105 (68%)
DAILY USE	40 (26%)	114 (74%)

ment was considered to be positive only if the outpatients attended the scheduled Outpatient Treatment Program four or more times or inpatients stayed the scheduled 30 days in the hospital. In Table III are listed the rates of engagement in treatment of patients classified according to marijuana use. There was no significant difference between any group classification and rates of engagement in treatment.

IV. Discussion

Recent cannabis use was evident in 30.5% of patients entering a drug-alcohol treatment program in Milwaukee by objective cannabinoid urinary detections. As expected, the higher prevalences were among the younger age groups. Therefore, it would appear

TABLE II

THC USE IN ALCOHOLICS
n=154

THC USE	AGE 13-19 n=21	20-24 n=18	25-29 n=34	30-39 n=45	40-49 n=21	50 n=15	EMPLOYED yes n=84	no n=70	SEX M n=110	F n=44	WHERE TREATED IP n=87	OP n=67	RACE W n=130	B n=18	Latin Amer. n=5	Native Amer. n=1	MARITAL STATUS Single n=61	Married n=59	Div. n=17	Sep. n=12	Div. n=5
+ URINE	11 (52%)	9 (50%)	11 (32%)	13 (29%)	3 (14%)	0 (0%)	21 (25%)	26 (37%)	34 (31%)	13 (28%)	29 (33%)	18 (27%)	36 (28%)	9 (50%)	1 (20%)	1 (100%)	29 (47%)	13 (22%)	3 (18%)	2 (17%)	0 (0%)
EVER	20 (95%)	14 (78%)	24 (71%)	25 (56%)	3 (14%)	2 (13%)	42 (49%)	46 (66%)	63 (57%)	25 (57%)	50 (57%)	38 (57%)	73 (56%)	12 (67%)	2 (40%)	1 (100%)	50 (82%)	23 (39%)	9 (53%)	6 (50%)	0 (0%)
RECENT	16 (76%)	10 (56%)	11 (32%)	12 (27%)	0 (0%)	0 (0%)	18 (21%)	31 (45%)	31 (28%)	18 (41%)	29 (33%)	20 (30%)	40 (31%)	8 (44%)	0 (0%)	1 (100%)	33 (54%)	11 (19%)	3 (18%)	2 (17%)	0 (0%)
DAILY	13 (62%)	9 (50%)	9 (27%)	9 (20%)	0 (0%)	0 (0%)	14 (16%)	26 (37%)	26 (24%)	14 (32%)	28 (32%)	12 (18%)	33 (25%)	6 (33%)	1 (20%)	0 (0%)	28 (46%)	9 (15%)	3 (18%)	0 (0%)	0 (0%)

TABLE III

Percent of Patients Engaged in
Treatment by THC Use

n (%) Engaged in Treatment

	n (%) Engaged in Treatment
Overall n=154	116 (75)
+ Urine THC n=47	33 (70)
- Urine THC n=107	83 (77)
+ Ever use THC n=88	65 (74)
- Ever use THC n=66	51 (77)
+ Recent use THC n=49	32 (65)
- Recent use THC n=105	84 (80)
+ Daily use THC n=40	26 (65)
- Daily use THC n=114	89 (78)

Engaged in treatment = having completed Inpatient treatment or having
attended a minimum of 4 Outpatient sessions.

that cannabis use was a sizeable problem among patients entering this treatment program, especially in the 14–20-year-olds where it was recently used by almost all.

The relatively close agreement between the rates of urinary detections and the histories of daily cannabis use suggests that historical information may be a reasonable estimate of the prevalence of cannabis use. However, these data from persons entering a drug and alcohol treatment program were obtained by skilled interviewers who should be able to elicit admissions of cannabis use efficiently. Also, the patients might be more free in their disclosures as they enter drug and alcohol abuse treatment than persons not entering treatment. It was noteworthy that there were relatively few who consistently denied recent cannabis use whose urines were positive for cannabinoid. Therefore, denial of cannabis use seemed much less prevalent among our patients insofar as we had been able to discover recent cannabis use. This is in contrast to some reports of the alcoholic patients underreporting alcohol use.[9] These data suggest that while alcoholics may minimize their alcohol intake, they are less reticent to acknowledge cannabis abuse patterns. These data do not support the routine use of a cannabinoid detection urinary screen in drug treatment centers. The cost does not seem warranted if adequate drug-use histories are elicited by competent interviewers. Marijuana use per se was not used as a criterion for admission to De Paul Rehabilitation Hospital. Admission criteria required the presence of some pharmacological or psychological problem related to drugs or problems at home, school, courts, or health related to drugs. There was no systematic difference in patient treatment related to the urinary detection of cannabinoids; nor were recent marijuana users treated differently from those without recent marijuana use. Patients who had used marijuana recently, as with other psychoactive drug use, were confronted with this finding and encouraged to abstain from it as well as other mood altering drugs.

The laboratory procedure used is considered specific for the cannabinoids and sufficiently sensitive to detect recent cannabis use up to ten days after last marijuana use. Therefore, a single urinary screen on admission can be considered a reasonable epidemiological tool to estimate prevalence of relatively recent cannabis use.

The rates of involvement of patients into the initial treatment process was apparently not notably affected by either the history or laboratory detection of recent cannabis use. This was surprising in the light of the common view that the polydrug abusers were more difficult to treat or enter into treatment than those whose drug abuse was of a single major psychoactive category.

Recent cannabis use was a quantitatively significant finding among alcohol abusing patients per se. Treatment components were included which were specifically directed towards eliminating its continuing use. It was not a major influence in the initial treatment involvement. The data do not imply that major modifications of an abstinence-oriented treatment program in relation to the discovery of cannabis use should follow that discovery in alcoholic patients entering treatment.

REFERENCES

1. AMA Council on Scientific Affairs. Marijuana: its health hazards and therapeutic potentials. JAMA, 1981; 243:1823-27.
2. Bernstein JG, Kuehnle JC, Mendelson JH. Medical implications of marihuana use. Am J Drug Alcohol Abuse, 1976; 3:347-61.
3. Nahas GG. Current status of marijuana research. JAMA, 1979; 24:2775-8.

4. Weller RA, Halikas JA. Objective criteria for the diagnosis of marijuana abuse. J Nervous and Mental Dis., 1980; 2:98-103.

5. Cohens S. The substance abuse problem. New York: Haworth Press, 1981.

6. Stimmel B, Korts D, Cohen M et al. Opiate addictions and alcoholism. Ann NY Acad Sci., 1981; 362:50-6.

7. Rowley GL, Armstrong, TA, Crowl, CP et al. Determination of THC and its metabolites by EMIT[R] homogeneous enzyme immunoussay—a summary report. In: Willette RE, ed, Cannabinoid assays in humans. NIDA Research Monograph 7, 1976, 28-32.

8. Johnston CD, Bachman JG, O'Malley PM. Student drug use in America 1975-1980. NIDA Division of Research, Rochelle, MD, 1981, 27-39.

9. Summers T. Validity of alcoholics' self-reported drinking history. Q. J. Stud. Alcohol., 1970; 31:972–4.

Alcohol Use during Pregnancy: What Advice Should Be Given to the Pregnant Woman?

David B. Roll, PhD
Terrence Smith, MPA
Elizabeth M. Whelan, ScD

ABSTRACT. There is no question that excessive alcohol use during pregnancy can harm the fetus. However, the available scientific evidence does not support the contention that absolute abstinence from alcohol is necessary to protect the unborn child. Pregnant women should be advised to limit alcohol intake, but a call for absolute abstinence is not justified, since such advice can have negative consequences. For example, it may lead women to equate real risks during pregnancy with hypothetical ones and might cause unnecessary anguish and guilt in women who had an occasional drink before their pregnancies were confirmed. Such women may even consider abortion, or hold themselves responsible for birth defects that have no relation to alcohol ingestion. Health scientists should be aware of the possible ramifications of their warnings and call for life-style changes only when truly required.

Introduction

During pregnancy, a woman is faced with many important and sometimes difficult choices. Recent scientific research has identified some life-style factors which may cause harm to the developing fetus. One such factor is the use of alcoholic beverages during pregnancy.

Since 1968, a growing body of scientific evidence has shown a relation between excessive alcohol use during pregnancy and birth defects. In an extreme form these abnormalities constitute the fetal

The authors are affiliated with the American Council on Science and Health. Address reprint requests to: Dr. Elizabeth M. Whelan, American Council on Science and Health, 1995 Broadway, New York, New York 10023.

alcohol syndrome (FAS), a condition described elsewhere in this volume.

Excessive consumption of alcohol during pregnancy is clearly hazardous to the health of the unborn child. Total abstinence, of course, will prevent all alcohol-related health problems. But the majority of American women drink to some extent and many want to know whether moderate drinking during pregnancy involves a risk to the unborn child.

There is no controversy that excessive alcohol ingestion causes FAS in some infants. Yet several important questions remain unanswered. These include whether:

—there is a threshold dose of alcohol which causes injury to the fetus,
—there is adequate information available to make meaningful recommendations to pregnant women concerning alcohol use,
—warnings based on less than satisfactory information do more harm than good.

Public Perception of Science

Despite our advanced and highly technological society, the public today is not very scientifically sophisticated. For example, John W. Hanley, Chairman of Monsanto Company, recently commented in a speech to the Association of American Medical Colleges: "In the past 10 years we have seen an alarming growth in what I would call an 'antiscience mentality,' particularly among those Americans who should know better—the ones with advanced education."[1]

He went on to note that in a recent survey conducted by the National Science Foundation, 42% described astrology as either "very scientific" or "sort of scientific." This was particularly true of younger adults. As a result of this inadequate training in science, some people are excessively fearful of many aspects of our environment, largely because they have difficulty separating scientific fact from fantasy.

The list of substances which have been subjects of public health warnings is long and spans several decades. Since the 1960s, to name a few, we have been warned about food additives (saccharin, cyclamate, nitrite), agricultural chemicals (DDT, the herbicide 2,4,5-T), hair dyes, spermicides, and aspirin. In many of these cases, early fears were not substantiated by later scientific evidence.

More recently, the possible health hazards of caffeine and alcohol use during pregnancy have achieved public notoriety, with federal government agencies leading the warning campaigns. It comes as no surprise that sometimes confusion reigns within the government. Recently, based on high dose animal studies, one federal agency warned pregnant women in rather strong terms that caffeine consumption during pregnancy might be associated with birth defects. Meanwhile, another agency continues to reprint and distribute a brochure on the effects of alcohol use during pregnancy illustrated with a picture of two pregnant women solemnly discussing the issue of alcohol—over a cup of coffee.[2]

Public health warnings should be based on fact, not on popular "wisdom," sensational press reports, or the desires of special interest groups. Whether the latter are so-called consumer advocacy organizations who insist on emphasizing only the potential harm of, for example, the chemicals with which we come into contact, or governmental regulatory agencies oversensitive to public or legislative criticism, both have an interest in self-perpetuation. One way of insuring that perpetuity is to reinforce the notion in the public mind that our bodies are constantly under the onslaught of poisonous chemicals that are carcinogens, mutagens, or teratogens. As a result, sometimes useful chemicals are banned unnecessarily. But the public feels protected, the agency or group has a continuing mandate and an illusion of progress in the battle against man-induced illness is fostered.

Certainly, we must have those who work to help ensure our health. Just as surely, the constant warnings to which the public is subjected tend to engender a fatalistic attitude in some people with regard to their own health. As author and scholar Lewis Thomas has said, "The new danger to our well-being, if we continue to listen to all the talk is in becoming a nation of healthy hypochondriacs, living gingerly, worrying ourselves half to death."[3] The litany of health risks makes it very difficult for the average person to distinguish real public health hazards from hypothetical ones.

Drinking during Pregnancy

In 1981, the Acting Surgeon General issued a warning that pregnant women should not only avoid alcoholic beverages, but also "be aware of the alcoholic content of food and drugs."[4] This advisory followed shortly after a government report to the President and Congress which summarized the information available about the health hazards of alcohol consumption.[5] In particular, this report dealt with the danger associated with alcohol ingestion during pregnancy. The report also acknowledged the unsatisfactory nature of the information available concerning the alleged effects of small amounts of alcohol on the fetus.

To date, there have been few well-controlled studies of humans regarding the effects of moderate alcohol consumption on pregnancy outcome. Two recent studies relate the effects of such alcohol ingestion to spontaneous abortion[6,7] and a third to decreased birth weight.[8]

The Surgeon General's warning is controversial among researchers in the field for a number of reasons, not the least of which is the continuing doubt among the above researchers as to the validity of their own results. For example, the authors of the most ambitious study,[6] which related alcohol use to spontaneous abortion in a population of 32,019 women, caution that they are unsure of the degree of under-reporting of alcohol use in their population. This study has also been criticized by others as under-reporting the number of heavy drinkers.[9] The authors of the second abortion study have been unable to confirm their earlier results and apparently are not too concerned about the effects of ingestion of modest amounts of alcohol by pregnant women, since one of the authors of this study has said, "Neither the birth weight findings nor the spontaneous abortion finding is so secure that women should feel guilty if they take a drink. As scientists, I don't think any of us believe that a little bit of alcohol causes these effects."[9]

The concern that moderate drinking may be associated with low birth weight is based on a 1977 study which indicated that the babies of women who said they consumed two drinks a day weighed 160 grams less than offspring of women who claimed to have drunk less.[8] It is not clear whether such an effect, if it exists, is of any clinical significance.

There are definite threshold effects in animals such as rats. That is, a dose exists below which there is no apparent effect on the fetus, and this dose is well above the equivalent of two drinks per day in humans.[9] Given this fact, one can only speculate as to the reasons for the abstinence recommendation by government bodies and some scientists. There has been a great deal of rhetoric, some of it bordering on the absurd. In fact, in one gross distortion of scientific data, alcohol has even been referred to as "Thalidomide II."[10] On the other hand, criticism of the abstinence recommendation has been made editorially by *The U.S. Journal of Drug and Alcohol Dependence.*[11]

Abstinence—An Effective Message?

Certainly it would be easier to say "don't drink." But in making that recommendation the questions must be asked whether such a warning does more harm than good and what impact this advice will have on its target audience. It is likely that the Surgeon General's call for abstinence will be taken seriously only by those who need it least if at all—light, social drinkers. Tragically, those women whose unborn children are at greatest risk of developing fetal alcohol syndrome are mostly chronic alcoholic women who are so ill it is doubtful that they could change their drinking habits without professional intervention.

Broad recommendations that people should modify their lifestyles in the pursuit of health should only be made if there is evidence that such modifications will have positive results. The reasoning of "it wouldn't hurt not to" is not only condescending but also unhelpful to people who simply want to know the facts.

Perhaps it is not asking too much for a woman to give up all alcoholic beverages during pregnancy. After all, she doesn't really "need it." This point of view, however, could be carried over into many other aspects of life. For example, what are the chances of her being involved in an automobile accident during pregnancy and thus risking miscarriage? Are all of her automobile rides really "necessary?" Of course, she may need to drive to work or to visit her obstetrician, but should she ride in a car to visit a friend or go to a movie, thus taking an "unnecessary" chance, however small? One could speculate about all sorts of small risks to which a pregnant woman submits herself everyday, risks that could be largely avoided, because she doesn't absolutely "need" to take them while pregnant.

Excessive health warnings may be counterproductive, and lead pregnant women to equate real risks during pregnancy (for example, cigarette smoking) with hypothetical risks (moderate use of alcohol). There should be a greater awareness on the part of public health professionals about the actual consequences of broad policy recommendations.

For example, a woman who was told that absolute abstinence from alcohol was necessary during pregnancy may unnecessarily worry about having had a drink or two each day before her pregnancy was confirmed. Ultimately, she might consider the option of abortion, fearing the birth of a deformed child when actually there is no scientific evidence for such a concern. Or consider the case of a woman who drank moderately during pregnancy and gave birth to a child with birth defects. In all likelihood, the defect had nothing to do with alcohol ingestion, and yet it is not difficult to imagine the mother blaming herself for her child's misfortune for the rest of her life. As health educators we must ask ourselves: Do we really want to be responsible for such a woman's guilt, based on the facts available to date? After a "sobering" look at the available data, we at the American Council on Science and Health have determined that we do not wish to take that responsibility.[12]

Recommendations

We believe the following recommendations to be those best supported by the available scientific evidence. They are conservative in that they recognize the potential risk inherent in excessive alcohol use during pregnancy. They also reflect a conscious attempt not to overstep the limitations of the existing data.

We recommend that during pregnancy a woman should:

—Discuss with her physician the risks of drinking, smoking, drug use, poor nutrition, and other potentially hazardous factors during pregnancy. Ideally, this should be done before pregnancy.

—Limit consumption of alcohol to no more than two drinks daily. This limit of one ounce of absolute alcohol daily is equivalent to two 12-ounce glasses of beer, two 4-ounce glasses of wine, or two mixed drinks each containing 1½ ounces of 80-proof liquor.

—Avoid substituting other drugs for alcohol to relieve tension or anxiety since some drugs may pose significant risks of their own.

—Particularly avoid "binge" drinking.

REFERENCES

1. Hanley JS. The antiscience mentality. Chem. and Eng. News, 1981; 5.
2. Alcohol and your unborn baby. Pub. No. PH-90, NIAAA, 5600 Fishers Lane, Rockville, MD 20857.
3. Thomas L. *The Medusa and the snail.* New York: The Viking Press, 1979:49.
4. Surgeon General's Advisory on Alcohol and Pregnancy. FDA Drug Bulletin, 1981; 11:9-10.
5. Report to the President and Congress on health hazards associated with alcohol and methods to inform the general public of these hazards. U.S. Department of the Treasury and U.S. Department of Health and Human Services, Nov. 1980.
6. Kline J, Shrout P, Stein Z, Susser M, Warburton D. Drinking during pregnancy and spontaneous abortion. Lancet, 1980; 2:176-80.
7. Harlap S, Shiono PH. Alcohol, smoking and incidence of spontaneous abortions in first and second trimester. Lancet, 1980; 2:173-6.
8. Little RE. Moderate alcohol use during pregnancy and decreased infant birth weight. Am J Public Health, 1977; 67:1154-6.
9. Kolata GB. Fetal alcohol advisory debated. Science, 1981; 214:642-5.
10. Enloe CE Jr. Thalidomide II. Nutrition Today, Jan/Feb 1982; 16-7.
11. Meddling with science. The U.S. Journal of Drug and Alcohol Dependence Jan.1982.
12. Alcohol use during pregnancy. American Council on Science and Health, 1995 Broadway, New York, N.Y., Dec. 1981.

Selective Guide
to Current Reference Sources
on Topics Discussed in this Issue

Theodora Andrews

1a. INDEXING AND ABSTRACTING TOOLS

Biological Abstracts. Philadelphia, Biosciences Information Service, 1926– , semimonthly.

Indexed by keywords from specific words appearing in titles plus added terms. Examples: Alcohol, Alcoholism, Alcoholics, Ethanol, Fetal alcohol syndrome, Mortality, Marihuana.

Chemical Abstracts. Columbus, OH, American Chemical Society, 1907– , weekly.

These are complicated searches. The Chemical Abstracts Service suggests that users when using cumulative indexes should first use the Index Guide volumes and their supplements, using the most recent supplement first. The Index Guide does not provide direct access to references in *Chemical Abstracts* but it guides the user to appropriate headings in the Chemical Substance and General Subject indexes. The best approach is probably to check under ''Ethanol'' to get registry number and suggestions for additional headings. Weekly issues contain keyword subject indexes.

Dissertation Abstracts International. A., Humanities and Social Sciences. Ann Arbor, MI, University Microfilms International, 1938– , monthly.

Since 1970 (vol. 30) keyword titles indexing has been provided as well as author. Search terms: Alcohol, Alcoholic, Alcoholism, Addiction, Mortality.

Dissertation Abstracts International. B., The Sciences and Engineering. Ann Arbor, MI, University Microfilms International, 1938– , monthly.

Theodora Andrews is Professor of Library Science, and Pharmacy, Nursing and Health Sciences Librarian, Purdue University, W. Lafayette, IN 47907.

Since 1970 (vol. 30) keyword title indexing has been provided as well as author. Search terms: Alcohol, Alcoholic, Alcoholism, Addiction, Mortality.

Excerpta Medica: Developmental Biology and Teratology. Section 21. Amsterdam, The Netherlands, Excerpta Medica, 1961– , 10 times per year.

Search terms: Alcohol, Alcoholism, Fetal alcohol syndrome.

Excerpta Medica: Drug Dependence. Section 40. Amsterdam, The Netherlands, Excerpta Medica, 1972– , monthly.

Search terms: Alcohol; Cannabis; Fetal alcohol syndrome; Teratogenicity therapy; Mortality, alcohol.

Excerpta Medica: Internal Medicine. Section 6. Amsterdam, The Netherlands, Excerpta Medica, 1947– , 20 times per year.

Search terms: Alcohol; Alcoholism; Ethanol; Fetal alcohol syndrome; Mortality, alcohol.

Excerpta Medica: Pharmacology and Toxicology. Section 30. Amsterdam, The Netherlands, Excerpta Medica, 1948– , 30 times per year.

Search terms: Alcohol, Alcoholism, Ethanol, Ethanol intake, Ethanol poisoning, Ethanol preference, Fetal alcohol syndrome, Cannabis.

Excerpta Medica: Public Health, Social Medicine, and Hygiene. Section 17. Amsterdam, The Netherlands, Excerpta Medica, 1955– , 20 times per year.

Search terms: Alcohol, Fetal alcohol syndrome, Fetus, Cannabis, Mortality, Depression.

Index Medicus (including *Bibliography of Medical Reviews*). Bethesda, MD, National Library of Medicine, 1960– , monthly.

Indexing terms are called *MeSH* terms. See: Alcohol drinking; Alcohol, ethyl; Alcoholic beverages; Alcoholic intoxication; Alcoholism; Psychoses, alcoholic; Fetal alcohol syndrome; Psychoses, substance-induced; Cannabis; Mortality; Therapeutic community; Depression.

NOTE: Indexing terms for the *Bibliography of Medical Reviews* are similar, except broader terms are used to enable grouping of similar material.

International Pharmaceutical Abstracts. Washington, DC, American Society of Hospital Pharmacists, 1964– , semimonthly.

Search terms: Alcoholism; Alcohols, ethyl; Cannabis.

Psychological Abstracts. Washington, DC, American Psychological Association, 1927– , monthly.

Search terms: Alcoholism, Marihuana, Depression, Group psychotherapy.

Psychopharmacology Abstracts. Rockville, MD, U.S. National Institute of Mental Health, 1961– , quarterly.

Search terms (from keywords in titles): Alcohol, Alcoholism, Ethanol, Marihuana, Cannabis, Depression, Fetal, Treatment.

Public Affairs Information Service Bulletin. New York, Public Affairs Information Service, 1915– , semimonthly.

Search terms: Alcoholism, Mortality, Marijuana.

Science Citation Index. Philadelphia, Institute for Scientific Information, 1961– , bimonthly.

Usually searched through citations, but has a "Permuterm Subject Index" generated from title words of source items indexed in the publication. Examples: Alcohol, Alcohol abuse, Alcohol consumption, Alcohol intoxication, and Ethanol with similar subheadings. To use the citation index look up name of author known to have published material relevant to the subject area of interest. Cited authors will be listed. Then use source index for complete description of articles found through the citation index.

Social Sciences Citation Index. Philadelphia, Institute for Scientific Information, 1973– , 3 times per year.

Similar to *Science Citation Index*. Search term examples: Alcoholics, Alcoholism, Depression, Marihuana, Cannabis.

Social Work Research and Abstracts. New York, National Association of Social Workers, 1965– , quarterly.

Search terms: Alcoholism, Alcoholism treatment programs, Group therapy, Depression.

Sociological Abstracts. San Diego, CA, International Sociological Association, 1953– , 5 times per year.

Search terms: Alcoholic, -s, -ism; Marijuana.

1b. ON-LINE BIBLIOGRAPHIC DATA BASES

ASI (American Statistics Index)
   A master guide and index to all statistical publications of the U.S. federal government.
BIOSIS PREVIEWS (Biological Abstracts and Biological Abstracts Reports, Reviews and Meetings)

A search guide is available. Keywords from titles and concept codes similar to those used in the printed index are used.

BOOKS IN PRINT (data base)

Contains bibliographic information on virtually the entire U.S. book publishing output. Includes: *A Subject Guide to Books in Print; Forthcoming Books; Scientific and Technical Books in Print;* and *Medical Books in Print.*

BOOKSINFO (BOOK)

Contains citations to more than 600,000 English language monographs currently in print from approximately 10,000 U.S. publishers (including academic and small presses) and 200 foreign publishers.

CA SEARCH *(Chemical Abstracts)*

The "Index Guide" which is used for searching the printed index should be utilized.

CHEMDEX/CHEMDEX2, CHEMDEX3

These files are dictionaries of all compounds cited in *Chemical Abstracts* since 1972. Each record describes a chemical substance by molecular formula, CAS Registry Number, CA Index Name, CAS Recognized Synonyms, and Full Ring Structure Information.

CHEMLINE *(The Chemical Dictionary On-Line)*

An interactive dictionary file created by the Specialized Information Services of the National Library of Medicine in collaboration with Chemical Abstracts Service. Provides a mechanism whereby over 1,000,000 chemical substance names and corresponding CAS Registry Numbers representing over 500,000 unique substances can be searched online.

COMPREHENSIVE DISSERTATION INDEX

A subject, title and author guide to American dissertations accepted at accredited institutions. Contents correspond to *Dissertation Abstracts International, American Doctoral Dissertations, Comprehensive Dissertation Index,* and *Master Abstracts.*

CONFERENCE PAPERS INDEX

A guide, *Conference Papers User Index Guide*, is available.

DRUG INFO/ALCOHOL USE: ABUSE (DRUG)

Contains citations from two different agencies: Druginfo Service Center, College of Pharmacy of the University of Minnesota, and the Hazeldon Foundation.

EXCERPTA MEDICA
   See: Excerpta Medica's *Guide to the Excerpta Medica Classification and Indexing System.* Search terms are those used in printed index sections, but everything is combined rather than treated in sections.
FOUNDATION DIRECTORY (Copyright Foundation Center)
   Is indexed by fields of interest. See: Alcoholism.
FOUNDATION GRANTS INDEX (Copyright Foundation Center)
   Subject access available.
GPO MONTHLY INDEX (Corresponds to *Monthly Catalogue of United States Government Publications*)
   Search terms the same as those used in printed version, such as Alcohol—physiological effect, Alcoholics, Alcoholism, and Alcoholism—treatment.
GRANTS
   Subject access available.
International Pharmaceutical Abstracts (IPA)
   Search terms are those used in the printed index, basically. A thesaurus is available.
ISI/BIOMED
   Biomedical disciplines worldwide are covered. Has a unique search capability not available in any other data base—direct access to the literature by research-front specialties.
MEDLINE (Medical Literature Analysis Retrieval System On-Line)
   Search terms are those used in the printed *Index Medicus* (MeSH).
MEDOC (Eccles Health Sciences Library, University of Utah produces. Covers government documents in health sciences.)
   MeSH subject headings used and keywords from titles.
MENTAL HEALTH ABSTRACTS (National Clearinghouse for Mental Health Information)
   All areas of mental health are covered.
NATIONAL FOUNDATIONS (Copyright Foundation Center)
   Indexed by activity code.
NTIS (National Technical Information Service)
   Several thesauri are used since material comes from a number of government agencies. Search terms include Alcohol consumption, Alcoholism, Alcohols.
PAIS INTERNATIONAL
   Corresponds to *Public Affairs Information Service Bulletin.*

Contains references to information in all fields of social sciences.

PRE-MED (Citations indexed PRE-vious to their appearance in MEDLINE)

Search terms are those used in *Index Medicus* (MeSH)

PRE-PSYCH

Begins with journals published in the Fall 1981. Citations appear within 4-8 weeks of their publication. Covers clinical psychology from 98 core psychological journals, and also psychological literature as it relates to criminal justice, the family, and education.

PSYCHINFO

Corresponds to the printed publication, *Psychological Abstracts.*

RTECS (Registry of Toxic Effects of Chemical Substances)

Search terms the same as those used in the printed version, e.g., Ethyl alcohol.

SCISEARCH

Indexed like the printed sources (*Science Citation Index* and *Current Contents*), that is, keywords from titles.

SOCIAL SCISEARCH

Indexed like the printed sources (*Social Sciences Citation Index* and *Current Contents*), that is, keywords from titles. Indexes significant items from 1,000 most important social sciences journals throughout the world and social sciences articles selected from about 2,200 additional journals in the natural, physical, and biomedical sciences.

SOCIOLOGICAL ABSTRACTS

Corresponds to the printed index.

SSIE Current Research (Smithsonian Science Information Exchange)

Guides are available: *SSIE Subject Indexes* and *SSIE Subject Terms and Synonyms.*

TDS (Toxicology Data Base)

A file of chemical, toxicological, and pharmacological facts extracted from standard reference sources. File may be searched by key words in titles, names of chemical substances, and by MeSH terms.

TOXLINE (Toxicology Information On-Line)

An extensive collection of bibliographic citations on human and animal toxicity, effects of environmental pollutants, adverse drug effects, and analytical methodology. File can be searched by key words in titles, and by words which indexer has added.

1c. BIBLIOGRAPHY OF BIBLIOGRAPHIES

Bibliographic Index. Bronx, NY, H. W. Wilson Co., 1937– , 3 times per year.

Search terms: Alcohol; Alcoholics; Alcoholism (with various sub-headings such as etiology, research, treatment, physiological effects, etc.)

1d. CURRENT AWARENESS PUBLICATIONS

Current Contents: Clinical Practice. Philadelphia, Institute for Scientific Information, 1973– , weekly.

Indexed by keywords from titles: examples: Alcohol; Alcohol - use; Alcoholism; Alcoholics; Alcohol consumption; Mortality; Depression.

Current Contents: Life Sciences. Philadelphia, Institute for Scientific Information, 1958– ,weekly.

Indexed by keywords from titles: examples: Alcohol; Alcohol consumption; Alcoholics; Alcoholism; Ethanol consumption; Mortality; Depression.

Current Contents: Social and Behavioral Sciences. Philadelphia, Institute for Scientific Information, 1969– , weekly.

Indexed by keywords from titles: examples: Alcohol, Alcohol abuse, Alcoholics, Alcoholism, Mortality, Depression.

Journal of Studies on Alcohol. Current Literature issues, published every other month.

Contains abstracts of current literature, new titles of current literature, and author and subject indexes. Search terms include: Fetal alcohol syndrome; Mortality; Alcoholism treatment; Group therapy, Multiple drug use, Depressions.

2. SOURCES OF NOTICES OF BOOKS, PERIODICALS, AND OTHER PUBLICATIONS

Andrews, Theodora. *A Bibliography of Drug Abuse, including Alcohol and Tobacco.* Littleton, CO, Libraries Unlimited, Inc., 1977.

Andrews, Theodora. *A Bibliography of Drug Abuse, Supplement 1977-1980.* Littleton, CO, Libraries Unlimited, Inc., 1981.
Critiques. Madison, WI, Wisconsin Clearinghouse for Alcohol and Other Drug Information, 1979– , bimonthly.
Irregular Serials and Annuals, 1983: An International Directory. 8th ed. New York, R. R. Bowker Co., 1982.
    Arranged by broad subjects; see: Drug abuse and alcoholism.
Medical Books and Serials in Print: An Index to Literature in the Health Sciences. New York, R. R. Bowker Co. Annual.
    Search terms: Alcohol in the body; Alcoholics; Alcoholism; Alcoholism - treatment; Mortality; Fetus abnormalities and deformities; Depression, mental.
National Library of Medicine Current Catalog. Bethesda, MD, U.S. National Library of Medicine, 1966– , quarterly.
    Search terms the same as those used in *Index Medicus* (MeSH).
Ulrich's International Periodicals Directory. 21st ed. New York, R. R. Bowker Co., 1982.
    Arranged by broad subjects; see: Drug abuse and alcoholism.
Journals that contain book reviews:
    Addictive Behaviors
    Addictive Diseases
    Alcohol Health and Research World
    British Journal on Alcohol and Alcoholism
    British Journal of Addiction to Alcohol
    Journal of Studies on Alcohol (Original articles issues)
See also in Section 1b, on-line bibliographic data bases BOOKS IN PRINT and BOOKSINFO (BOOK)

3. U.S. GOVERNMENT PUBLICATIONS

Government Reports Announcements and Index. Springfield, VA, National Technical Information Service. Biweekly.
    Contains a biological and medical sciences section, further subdivided. Has a keyword index of words selected from a controlled vocabulary of terms. Examples: Alcoholic beverages, Alcoholism.
Monthly Catalog of United States Government Publications. Washington, DC, U.S. Government Printing Office. Monthly.

4. SOURCES OF INFORMATION ON GRANTS

Annual Register of Grant Support. Chicago, Marquis Academic Media. Annual.
   Has a section on life sciences and indexes by subject, organization and program, geographic area, and personnel.
Directory of Research Grants. Scottsdale, AZ, Oryx Press, 1981 ed.
   Is arranged by subject. See: Alcoholism.
Foundation Grants Index. Edited by Lee Noe et al. New York, Foundation Center. Annual.
   Has a subject index.
NIH Guide for Grants and Contracts. Washington, DC, U.S. Department of Health and Human Services.
   Published at irregular intervals to announce scientific initiatives and to provide policy and administrative information to individuals and organizations who need to be kept informed of opportunities, requirements, and changes in grants and contracts activities administered by the National Institutes of Health.

5. GUIDES TO UPCOMING MEETINGS

World Meetings: Medicine. New York, Macmillan Publishing Co. Quarterly.
   See: Keyword subject index, sponsor directory, and index.

6. PROCEEDINGS OF MEETINGS

Conference Papers Index. Louisville, KY, Data Courier, Inc., 1973– , monthly.
Index of Conference Proceedings Received. The British Library, Lending Division, 1964– , monthly with annual, 5 and 10 year cumulations.
   Search terms: Alcohol, Alcohol abuse, Alcohol studies, Alcoholism.
Index to Scientific and Technical Proceedings. Philadelphia, Institute for Scientific Information, 1978– , monthly (Semi-annual cumulations).
   Has Permuterm^R (keyword) subject and other indexes.

InterDok Directory of Published Proceedings. White Plains, NY, InterDok Corp., 1965– , monthly except July-Aug.; annual cumulations.

> Principal indexing is by keyword in the name of the conference and the titles. Also has a sponsor index.

7. MISCELLANEOUS RELEVANT PUBLICATIONS

Alcoholism and Alcohol Abuse among Women: Research Issues. Proceedings of a workshop, April 2-5, 1978. Jekyll Island, GA, sponsored by the Division of Extramural Research, U.S. National Institute on Alcohol Abuse and Alcoholism. (NIAAA Research Monograph No.1; DHEW Publication No. ADM 80-835.) Washington, DC, U.S. GPO, 1980.

> Of value in alcohol research in that it represents the major thinking prior to 1978.

Drug and Alcohol Abuse: Implications for Treatment. Edited by Stephen E. Gardner. Rockville, MD, U.S. Dept. of Health and Human Services, Public Health Service, Alcohol, Drug Abuse and Mental Health Administration, National Institute on Drug Abuse. (Treatment Research Monograph Series, DHHS Publication No. ADM 80-958.) Washington, DC, U.S. GPO, 1981.

> Addresses the combined use of drugs and alcohol.

Iowa Drug Information Service (IDIS). Iowa City, Iowa, University of Iowa College of Pharmacy. 1965– .

> Microfiche file. Subscribers may request computer search of data base. Search terms: Alcohol; Alcohol toxicity; Cannabinoids.

Registry of Toxic Effects of Chemical Substances. 1980 ed. 2 v. Cincinnati, U.S. Center for Disease Control, National Institute for Occupational Safety and Health, 1982.

> Key words: Ethyl alcohol, Cannabis.

U.S. National Institute on Alcohol Abuse and Alcoholism. *First Statistical Compendium on Alcohol and Health.* Washington, DC, U.S. GPO, 1981.

> Pulls together materials from Rutgers, the National Clearinghouse for Alcohol Information, the NIAAA Alcohol Epidemiological Data System, the National Alcoholism Program Information System (NAPIS), and State Alcoholism Program Information System files (SAPIS), NIAAA surveys and grants and contract reports, and other data.

U.S. National Institute on Alcohol Abuse and Alcoholism. *National Status Report. State Alcoholism Profile Information System (SAPIS)*. Rockville, MD, NIAAA, 1982. An important source of information.

U.S. National Institute on Alcohol Abuse and Alcoholism. *Third Special Report to the U.S. Congress on Alcohol and Health*. From the Secretary of Health, Education and Welfare. Edited by Ernest P. Noble. (DHEW Publication No. ADM 78-569.) Washington, DC, U.S. GPO, 1978. Incorporates the most significant findings from research in the alcoholism field.

Vuosikirja Arsbok = Alcohol Statistics. Oy Alko Ab. Helsinki, Finland, Oy Alko Ab. Annual. Text in Finnish and Swedish; summaries in English. Provides information on production, imports, and sales of alcohol containing substances, the consumption and prices of alcoholic beverages, detrimental effects of alcohol, and control measures. Most data concern Finland.

8. SPECIAL LIBRARIES WITH COLLECTIONS OF NOTE

Alcoholism and Drug Addiction Research Foundation Library, 33 Russell St., Toronto, Ontario M5S 2S1, Canada.

Rutgers University Center of Alcohol Studies Library. Smithers Hall, Busch Campus, New Brunswick, NJ 08903.

Information for Authors

Advances in Alcohol & Substance Abuse publishes original articles and topical review articles related to all areas of substance abuse. Each publication will be issue-oriented and may contain both basic science and clinical papers. All submitted manuscripts are read by the editors. Many manuscripts may be further reviewed by consultants. Comments from reviewers will be returned with the rejected manuscripts when it is believed that this may be helpful to the author(s).

The content of *Advances in Alcohol & Substance Abuse* is protected by copyright. Manuscripts are accepted for consideration with the understanding that their contents, all or in part, have not been published elsewhere and will not be published elsewhere except in abstract form or with the express consent of the editor. Author(s) of accepted manuscripts will receive a form to sign for transfer of author's(s') copyright.

The editor reserves the right to make those revisions necessary to achieve maximum clarity and conciseness as well as uniformity to style. *Advances in Alcohol & Substance Abuse* accepts no responsibility for statements made by contributing author(s).

MANUSCRIPT PREPARATION

A double-spaced original and two copies (including references, legends, and footnotes) should be submitted. The manuscript should have margins of at least 4 cm, with subheadings used at appropriate intervals to aid in presentation. There is no definite limitation on length, although a range of fifteen to twenty typed pages is desired.

A cover letter should accompany the manuscript containing the name, address, and phone number of the individual who will be specifically responsible for correspondence.

Title Page

The first page should include title, subtitle (if any), first name, and last name of each author, with the highest academic degree obtained. Each author's academic and program affiliation(s) should be noted, including the name of the department(s) and institution(s) to which the work should be attributed; disclaimers (if any); and the name and address of the author to whom reprint requests should be addressed. Any acknowledgements of financial support should also be listed.

Abstracts

The second page should contain an abstract of not more than 150 words.

References

References should be typed double space on separate pages and arranged according to their order in the text. In the text the references should be in superscript arabic numerals. The form of references should conform to the Index Medicus (National Library of Medicine) style. Sample references are illustrated below:

1. Brown MJ, Salmon D, Rendell M. Clonidine hallucinations. Ann Intern Med. 1980; 93:456–7.
2. Friedman HJ, Lester D. A critical review of progress towards an animal model of alcoholism. In: Blum K, ed. Alcohol and opiates: neurochemical and behavioral mechanisms. New York: Academic Press, 1977:1–19.
3. Berne E. Principles of group treatment. New York: Oxford University Press, 1966.

Reference to articles in press must state name of journal and, if possible, volume and year. References to unpublished material should be so indicated in parentheses in the text.

It is the responsibility of the author(s) to check references against the original source for accuracy both in manuscript and in galley proofs.

Tables and Figures

Tables and figures should be unquestionably clear so that their meaning is understandable without the text. Tables should be typed double space on separate sheets with number and title. Symbols for units should be confined to column headings. Internal, horizontal, and vertical lines may be omitted. The following footnote symbols should be used: * † ‡ § ¶

Figures should be submitted as glossy print photos, untrimmed and unmounted. The label pasted on the back of each illustration should contain the name(s) of author(s) and figure number, with top of figure being so indicated. Photomicrographs should have internal scale markers, with the original magnification as well as stain being used noted. If figures are of patients, the identities should be masked or a copy of permission for publication included. If the figure has been previously published, permission must be obtained from the previous author(s) and copyright holder(s). Color illustrations cannot be published.

Manuscripts and other communications should be addressed to:

Barry Stimmel, MD
Mount Sinai School of Medicine
One Gustave L. Levy Place
Annenberg 5-12
New York, New York 10029